ACTIVE PHYSICS

Arthur Eisenkraft, Ph.D.

Active Physics has been developed in association
with the
American Association of Physics Teachers (AAPT)
and the
American Institute of Physics (AIP)

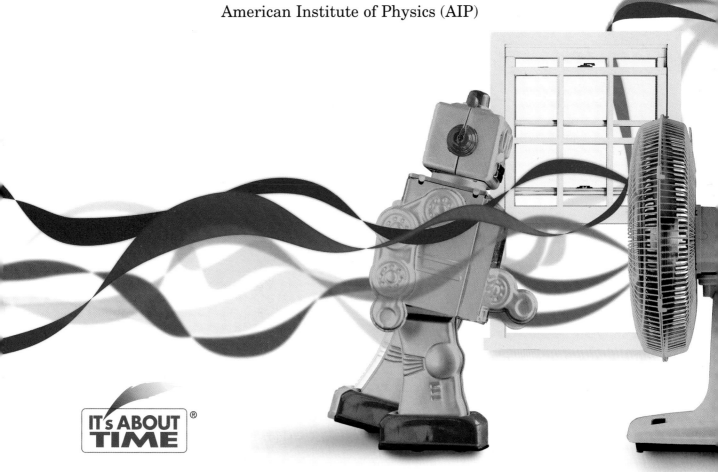

IT'S ABOUT TIME ®

Published by
IT'S ABOUT TIME, Inc.
Armonk, NY

Published in 1998 by

It's About Time, Inc.

84 Business Park Drive, Armonk, NY 10504
Phone (914) 273-2233 Fax (914) 273-2227
Toll Free (888) 698-TIME
http://Its-About-Time.com

Publisher
Laurie Kreindler

Project Manager
Ruta Demery

Design
John Nordland

Production Manager
Barbara Zahm

Creative Artwork
Tomas Bunk

Cover Illustration
Steven Belcher

Production
Spinning Egg Design Group, Inc.

Technical Art
Burmar

Illustrations and Photos

Chapter 1: Tomas Bunk pages 8, 19, 24, 29, 33, 37; PhotoDisc Inc. pages 1-4, 7, 9, 11, 13, 17-18, 21, 23 26, 28, 30, 32, 34, 36, 40, 42; Amla Sanghvi page 4 (lower right); Micheal Simpson/FPG International LLC page 5; The Home Depot page 27; **Chapter 2:** Tomas Bunk pages 46, 50, 55, 60, 64, 74, 79; PhotoDisc Inc. pages 43-45, 47, 49, 53-54, 56, 62, 66, 71, 78, 80, 82, 84; KRUPS, Inc. page 58; **Chapter 3:** Tomas Bunk pages 88, 93, 109, 113; PhotoDisc Inc. pages 85-87, 91-92, 94, 96, 99, 102, 108, 110, 112, 117.

All student activities in this textbook have been designed to be as safe as possible, and have been reviewed by professionals specifically for that purpose. As well, appropriate warnings concerning potential safety hazards are included where applicable to particular activities. However, responsibility for safety remains with the student, the classroom teacher, the school principal, and the school board.

Printed and bound in the United States of America
ISBN 1-891629-01-8

1 2 3 4 5 D 02 01 00 99 98

This project was supported, in part,
by the
National Science Foundation
Opinions expressed are those of the authors
and not necessarily those of the Foundation

Home
Table of Contents

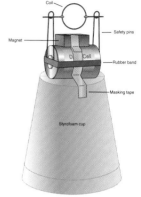

Acknowledgments

Project Director

Arthur Eisenkraft teaches physics and serves as science coordinator in the Bedford Public Schools in N.Y. Dr. Eisenkraft is the author of numerous science and educational publications. He holds a US Patent for a laser vision testing system and was featured in *Scientific American*.

Dr. Eisenkraft is chair of the Duracell Science Scholarship Competition; chair of the Toyota TAPESTRY program giving grants to science teachers; and chair of the Toshiba/NSTA ExploraVisions Awards competition for grades K-12. He is co-author of a contest column and serves on the advisory board of *Quantum* magazine, a collaborative effort of the US and Russia. In 1993, he served as Executive Director for the XXIV International Physics Olympiad after being Academic Director for the United States Team for six years. He served on the content committee and helped write the National Science Education Standards of the NRC (National Research Council).

Dr. Eisenkraft received the Presidential Award for Excellence in Science Teaching at the White House in 1986, and the AAPT Distinguished Service Citation for "excellent contributions to the teaching of physics" in 1989. In 1991 he was recognized by the Disney Corporation as Science Teacher of the Year in their American Teacher Awards program. In 1993 he received an Honorary Doctor of Science degree from Rensselaer Polytechnic Institute.

Primary and Contributing Authors

Home

Jon L. Harkness
Active Physics Regional Coordinator
Wausau, WI

Douglas A. Johnson
Madison West High School
Madison, WI

John J. Rusch
University of Wisconsin, Superior
Superior, WI

Ruta Demery
Blue Ink Editing
Stayner, ON

Communications

Richard Berg
University of Maryland
College Park, MD

Ron DeFronzo
Eastbay Ed. Collaborative
Attleboro, MA

Harry Rheam
Eastern Senior High School
Atco, NJ

John Roeder
The Calhoun School
New York, NY

Patty Rourke
Potomac School
McLean, VA

Larry Weathers
The Bromfield School
Harvard, MA

Medicine

Russell Hobbie
University of Minnesota
St. Paul, MN

Terry Goerke
Hill-Murray High School
St. Paul, MN

John Koser
Wayzata High School
Plymouth, MN

Ed Lee
WonderScience, Associate Editor
Silver Spring, MD

Predictions

Ruth Howes
Ball State University
Muncie, IN

Chris Chiaverina
New Trier Township High School
Crystal Lake, IL

Charles Payne
Ball State University
Muncie, IN

Ceanne Tzimopoulos
Omega Publishing
Medford, MA

Sports

Howard Brody
University of Pennsylvania
Philadelphia, PA

Mary Quinlan
Radnor High School
Radnor, PA

Carl Duzen
Lower Merion High School
Havertown, PA

Jon L. Harkness
Active Physics Regional Coordinator
Wausau, WI

David Wright
Tidewater Comm. College
Virginia Beach, VA

Transportation

Ernest Kuehl
Lawrence High School
Cedarhurst, NY

Robert L. Lehrman
Bayside, NY

Salvatore Levy
Roslyn High School
Roslyn, NY

Tom Liao
SUNY Stony Brook
Stony Brook, NY

Bob Ritter
University of Alberta
Edmonton, AB, CA

Principal Investigators

Bernard V. Khoury
American Association of Physics Teachers

Dwight Edward Neuenschwander
American Institute of Physics

Consultants

Peter Brancazio
Brooklyn College of CUNY
Brooklyn, NY

Robert Capen
Canyon del Oro High School
Tucson, AZ

Carole Escobar

Earl Graf
SUNY Stony Brook
Stony Brook, NY

Jack Hehn
American Association of
Physics Teachers
College Park, MD

Donald F. Kirwan
Louisiana State University
Baton Rouge, LA

Gayle Kirwan
Louisiana State University
Baton Rouge, LA

James La Porte
Virginia Tech
Blacksburg, VA

Charles Misner
University of Maryland
College Park, MD

Robert F. Neff
Suffern, NY

Ingrid Novodvorsky
Mountain View High School
Tucson, AZ

John Robson
University of Arizona
Tucson, AZ

Mark Sanders
Virginia Tech
Blacksburg, VA

Brian Schwartz
Brooklyn College of CUNY
New York, NY

Bruce Seiger
Wellesley High School
Newburyport, MA

Clifford Swartz
SUNY Stony Brook
Setauket, NY

Barbara Tinker
The Concord Consortium
Concord, MA

Robert E. Tinker
The Concord Consortium
Concord, MA

Joyce Weiskopf
Herndon, VA

Donna Willis
American Association of
Physics Teachers
College Park, MD

Safety Reviewer

Gregory Puskar
University of West Virginia
Morgantown, WV

Equity Reviewer

Leo Edwards
Fayettville State University
Fayettville, NC

Spreadsheet and MBL

Ken Appel
Yorktown High School
Peekskill, NY

Physics at Work

Barbara Zahm
Zahm Productions
New York, NY

Physics InfoMall

Brian Adrian
Bethany College
Lindsborg, KS

Unit Reviewers

George A. Amann
F.D. Roosevelt High School
Rhinebeck, NY

Patrick Callahan
Catasaugua High School
Center Valley, PA

Beverly Cannon
Science and Engineering
Magnet High School
Dallas, TX

Barbara Chauvin

Elizabeth Chesick
The Baldwin School
Haverford, PA 19041

Chris Chiaverina
New Trier Township High School
Crystal Lake, IL

Andria Erzberger
Palo Alto Senior High School
Los Altos Hills, CA

Elizabeth Farrell Ramseyer
Niles West High School
Skokie, IL

Mary Gromko
President of Council of State
Science Supervisors
Denver, CO

Thomas Guetzloff

Jon L. Harkness
Active Physics Regional Coordinator
Wausau, WI

Dawn Harman
Moon Valley High School
Phoenix, AZ

James Hill
Piner High School
Sonoma, CA

Bob Kearney

Claudia Khourey-Bowers
McKinley Senior High School

Steve Kliewer
Bullard High School
Fresno, CA

Ernest Kuehl
Roslyn High School
Cedarhurst, NY

Jane Nelson
University High School
Orlando, FL

John Roeder
The Calhoun School
New York, NY

Patty Rourke
Potomac School
McLean, VA

Gerhard Salinger
Fairfax, VA

Irene Slater
La Pietra School for Girls

Pilot Test Teachers

John Agosta

Donald Campbell
Portage Central High School
Portage, MI

John Carlson
Norwalk Community
Technical College
Norwalk, CT

Veanna Crawford
Alamo Heights High School
New Braunfels

Janie Edmonds
West Milford High School
Randolph, NJ

Eddie Edwards
Amarillo Area Center for
Advanced Learning
Amarillo, TX

Arthur Eisenkraft
Fox Lane High School
Ossining, NY

Tom Ford

Bill Franklin

Roger Goerke
St. Paul, MN

Tom Gordon
Greenwich High School
White Plains, NY

Ariel Hepp

John Herrman
College of Steubenville
Steubenville, OH

Linda Hodges

Ernest Kuehl
Lawrence High School
Cedarhurst, NY

Fran Leary
Troy High School
Schenectady, NY

Harold Lefcourt

Cherie Lehman
West Lafayette High School
West Lafayette, IN

Kathy Malone
Shady Side Academy
Pittsburgh, PA

Bill Metzler
Westlake High School
Thornwood, NY

Elizabeth Farrell Ramseyer
Niles West High School
Skokie, IL

Daniel Repogle
Central Noble High School
Albion, IN

Evelyn Restivo
Maypearl High School
Maypearl, TX

Doug Rich
Fox Lane High School
Bedford, NY

John Roeder
The Calhoun School
New York, NY

Tom Senior
New Trier Township High School
Highland Park, IL

John Thayer
District of Columbia Public Schools
Silver Spring, MD

Carol-Ann Tripp
Providence Country Day
East Providence, RI

Yvette Van Hise
High Tech High School
Freehold, NJ

Jan Waarvick

Sandra Walton
Dubuque Senior High School
Dubuque, IA

Larry Wood
Fox Lane High School
Bedford, NY

Field Test Coordinator

Marilyn Decker
Northeastern University
Acton, MA

Field Test Workshop Staff

John Carlson

Marilyn Decker

Arthur Eisenkraft

Douglas Johnson

John Koser

Ernest Kuehl

Mary Quinlan

Elizabeth Farrell Ramseyer

John Roeder

Field Test Evaluators

Susan Baker-Cohen

Susan Cloutier

George Hein

Judith Kelley

all from Lesley College,
Cambridge, MA

Field Test Teachers and Schools

Rob Adams
Polytech High School
Woodside, DE

Benjamin Allen
Falls Church High School
Falls Church, VA

Robert Applebaum
New Trier High School
Winnetka, IL

Joe Arnett
Plano Sr. High School
Plano, TX

Bix Baker
GFW High School
Winthrop, MN

Debra Beightol
Fremont High School
Fremont, NE

Patrick Callahan
Catasaugua High School
Catasaugua, PA

George Coker
Bowling Green High School
Bowling Green, KY

Janice Costabile
South Brunswick High School
Monmouth Junction, NJ

Stanley Crum
Homestead High School
Fort Wayne, IN

Russel Davison
Brandon High School
Brandon, FL

Christine K. Deyo
Rochester Adams High School
Rochester Hills, MI

Jim Doller
Fox Lane High School
Bedford, NY

Jessica Downing
Esparto High School
Esparto, CA

Douglas Fackelman
Brighton High School
Brighton, CO

Rick Forrest
Rochester High School
Rochester Hills, MI

Mark Freeman
Blacksburg High School
Blacksburg, VA

Jonathan Gillis
Enloe High School
Raleigh, NC

Karen Gruner
Holton Arms School
Bethesda, MD

Larry Harrison
DuPont Manual High School
Louisville, KY

Alan Haught
Weaver High School
Hartford, CT

Steven Iona
Horizon High School
Thornton, CO

Phil Jowell
Oak Ridge High School
Conroe, TX

Deborah Knight
Windsor Forest High School
Savannah, GA

Thomas Kobilarcik
Marist High School
Chicago, IL

Sheila Kolb
Plano Senior High School
Plano, TX

Todd Lindsay
Park Hill High School
Kansas City, MO

Malinda Mann
South Putnam High School
Greencastle, IN

Steve Martin
Maricopa High School
Maricopa, AZ

Nancy McGrory
North Quincy High School
N. Quincy, MA

David Morton
Mountain Valley High School
Rumford, ME

Charles Muller
Highland Park High School
Highland Park, NJ

Fred Muller
Mercy High School
Burlingame, CA

Vivian O'Brien
Plymouth Regional High School
Plymouth, NH

Robin Parkinson
Northridge High School
Layton, UT

Donald Perry
Newport High School
Bellevue, WA

Francis Poodry
Lincoln High School
Philadelphia, PA

John Potts
Custer County District High School
Miles City, MT

Doug Rich
Fox Lane High School
Bedford, NY

John Roeder
The Calhoun School
New York, NY

Consuelo Rogers
Maryknoll Schools
Honolulu, HI

Lee Rossmaessler, Ph.D
Mott Middle College High School
Flint, MI

John Rowe
Hughes Alternative Center
Cincinnati, OH

Rebecca Bonner Sanders
South Brunswick High School
Monmouth Junction, NJ

David Schlipp
Narbonne High School
Harbor City, CA

Eric Shackelford
Notre Dame High School
Sherman Oaks, CA

Robert Sorensen
Springville-Griffith Institute and
Central School
Springville, NY

Teresa Stalions
Crittenden County High School
Marion, KY

Roberta Tanner
Loveland High School
Loveland, CO

Anthony Umelo
Anacostia Sr. High School
Washington, D.C.

Judy Vondruska
Mitchell High School
Mitchell, SD

Deborah Waldron
Yorktown High School
Arlington, VA

Ken Wester
The Mississippi School for
Mathematics and Science
Columbus, MS

Susan Willis
Conroe High School
Conroe, TX

You can do physics. Here are the reasons why.

The following features make it that much easier to understand the physics principles you will be studying. Using all these features together will help you actually learn about this subject and see how it works for you everyday, everywhere. Look for all these features in each chapter of Active Physics.

2 Challenge

This feature presents the problem you will soon be expected to solve, or the tasks you are expected to complete using the knowledge you gain in the chapter.

3 Criteria

Before the chapter begins you will learn exactly how you will be graded. Working with your classmates, you will even help determine the criteria by which your work will be evaluated.

1 Scenario

Each unit begins with a realistic event or situation you might actually have experienced, or can imagine yourself participating in at home, in school, or in your community.

4 What Do You Think?

What do you already know? This unique feature encourages you to explore and discuss the ideas you have on a topic before you begin studying it.

5 For You to Do

In Active Physics you learn by doing. Activities encourage you to work through problems by yourself, in small groups, or with the whole class.

6 Physics Talk

When you come across a physics term or equation in the chapter that you may not be familiar with, turn to this feature for a useful, easy-to-understand explanation.

7 For You to Read

In this feature you will find additional insight, or perhaps an interesting new perspective into the topic of the activity.

8 Reflecting on the Activity and the Challenge

Each activity helps prepare you to be successful in the chapter challenge. This feature helps you relate this activity to the larger challenge. It's another piece of the chapter jigsaw puzzle.

9 Physics to Go

Here are exercises, problems, and questions that help you further develop your understanding of the activity and relate it to the chapter challenge.

10 Inquiry Investigation

You are given an opportunity to design your own investigation using the skills you have acquired in the activities.

11 Stretching Exercises

If you're looking for more challenging or in-depth problems, questions, and exercises, you'll find them right here.

12 Chapter Assessment

How do you measure up? Here is your opportunity to share what you have actually learned. Using the activities as a guide, you can now complete the challenge you were presented at the beginning of the chapter.

13 Physics You Learned

This lists the physics terms, principles, and skills you have just learned in the chapter.

14 Physics at Work

Using real people in real jobs, this feature demonstrates how the principles you are learning are being applied everyday, everywhere. It shows that people who use physics can make a difference.

Imagine meeting someone who never heard of your favorite movie or music group! Now imagine how enriched they would be if they could enjoy that movie or music the way you do.

Active Physics came about as a result of a similar frustration. The usual physics course has so much math and so much reading that many students miss the beauty, the excitement, and the usefulness of physics. Many more students simply refuse to take the course. Active Physics began when a group of physicists and physics teachers wondered how to pass on their enjoyment of physics to high school students.

Physics should be experienced and make sense to you. Each chapter of Active Physics begins with a challenge—develop a sport that can be played on the Moon; build a home for people with a housing crisis; pursuade your parents to lend you the family car; and so on. These are tough challenges, but you will learn the physics that will allow you to be successful at every one.

Part of your education is to learn to trust yourself and to question others. When someone tells you something, can they answer your questions: "How do you know? Why should I believe you? and Why should I care?" After Active Physics, when you describe why seatbelts are important, or why loud music can be hazardous, or why communication with extraterrestrials is difficult, and someone asks, "How do you know?" your answer will be, "I know because I did an experiment."

Only a small number of high school students study physics. You are already a part of this select group. Physics awaits your discovery. Enjoy the journey.

Arthur Eisenkraft

DESIGNING THE
UNIVERSAL DWELLING

CHAPTER
1

Helping people is great. However, history is filled with stories of individuals who have tried to make changes without any respect for the people they are helping or their culture.

In this *Active Physics* chapter you will design a prototype home that can be used in many different areas of the world where housing crises have emerged. If you were to be involved in such a project, it would be important for you to work together with the people you are helping in assessing their needs, and their capabilities. Although that is not possible given your limited time, you should recognize the need for this type of collaborative teamwork when assisting people.

Scenario

Imagine you and your team members are part of an international group called Homes For Everyone (HFE). The purpose of your organization is to address the growing housing shortage in many areas throughout the world. You have recently been sent to work with a self-help community group in a far-away area. Here is a letter you might write home.

Dear Mom and Dad,

Greetings! I've finally settled into my new home. Sometimes I think that I'm not in another country but on another planet. Everything here is so different. Sorry about the water splotches on this letter. It's pouring rain outside, and the roof is leaking. I have to remind myself that at least I have a roof over my head. Many people here have lost their homes from the last hurricane and are crowded into their relatives' already crowded spaces.

We're trying to figure out what we can do to help with the housing situation here. We're still not sure what the solution is. Right now I'm trying to learn more about these people who have been so generous and gracious to me. When we arrived the whole village got together to greet our group. I felt so honored! I expect the same kind of welcome from my family when I return home!

Tomorrow we are going to start looking around. I'll keep you posted on what we discover and on our progress. Signing off for now. Miss you all!

Love,

Kim

HFE plans to design a "universal" dwelling to meet the need for homes in diverse environments. The group needs a design that can be constructed quickly and simply at the building site. The design should also use the least amount of materials to create the most living space. To make mass production possible, the dwelling design should be uniform, but you should be able to make simple changes to meet local conditions. It should be energy efficient in any climate.

Challenge

After completing the eight activities in this chapter you will be challenged to do the following to present to the HFE Architectural Committee;

1. Develop scale drawings of the floor plan and all side views of the universal dwelling. Following are specifications for the drawings:

    a) The drawings should be done on a scale of 1 inch = 4 feet (1:48).

    b) The scale drawings should include all sides of the house, showing roof lines, roof overhangs, and placement and dimensions of all windows for a selected climactic region and culture.

    c) The scale drawings should show the floor plans of the living spaces and include specifications for the thickness of the wall, types of insulation and their thickness, and kinds and types of windows or ventilation openings.

    d) The plans should show the geographic orientation of the house (in which direction the house should face).

2. Write a two-page explanation which gives your reasons for the following:

    a) your choices for the shape and dimensions of the dwelling,

    b) the energy consideration that went into the design of the dwelling,

    c) the changes that could be made to the basic design to take into account different climates and cultures,

    d) the things you included to make your dwelling attractive.

Criteria for Evaluation

The HFE Architectural Committee will use criteria similiar to the ones below in evaluating your drawings and your written presentation. Discuss and decide as a class the exact criteria the committee should use.

- **(20%) The drawings and written presentation should meet all specifications listed in the Challenge.**

- **(10%) The drawings and written presentation should explain how you considered surface-to-volume ratio in your design.**

- **(20%) The written presentation should explain how the house will accommodate differing seasonal and climactic conditions in terms of heating and cooling. It should also show you have a basis for scaling the dwelling appropriate to the family and culture for which it is designed.**

- **(20%) The design of the roof and the placement and dimensions of windows should account for climactic, solar, and latitude considerations, and should show you have accounted for the advantages and disadvantages of windows.**

- **(20%) The placement and kind of insulation materials and thickness you choose should show you know the principles which make insulation effective.**

- **(10%) The appearance of your house and the interior layout should show consideration for fundamental human needs.**

Activity One

Factors in Designing the "Universal" Dwelling

WHAT DO YOU THINK?

All humans have a basic need for shelter. Examine the pictures of dwellings shown on this page.

- **What are some common characteristics of all these dwellings?**
- **How are they alike? How are they different?**

Record your ideas about these questions in your *Active Physics log*. Be prepared to discuss your reponses with your small group and the class.

FOR YOU TO DO

1. "Brainstorming" is a process in which you simply generate a large number of ideas. The rule of brainstorming is that all ideas should be accepted and no idea should be evaluated or thrown out. With your group, brainstorm a list of the characteristics of a "universal dwelling" for people anywhere in the world. In this case, set your team's goal at 100 different characteristics. Use the following questions to guide your brainstorming.

  a) What are the functions of a home?

  b) What features are essential to any home?

  c) What are some of the factors that determine the size and shape of a home?

2. After brainstorming, narrow the lists down and develop two lists of ten or less items each. The first list should identify essential characteristics that should be present in all homes. The second list should identify special characteristics that are absolutely necessary for some environments, but that are non-essential in other environments.

  a) Record the lists in your log using these two headings:

    • Essential characteristics of the universal dwelling.
    • Characteristics that must be modified for various climactic and cultural conditions.

3. Return to your group and answer the following questions in your log:

  a) What things do you need to know about people, family sizes, and lifestyles in order to design a universal dwelling?

  b) How large should a universal dwelling be? How could you make an educated guess?

  c) How many of your "essential characteristics of the universal dwelling" require an energy input of some kind?

REFLECTING ON THE ACTIVITY AND CHALLENGE

You may think that this activity didn't move you very far toward meeting the challenge, but it really has gotten you started. Through interaction with others you have identified and shared ideas about the two basic aspects of dwellings for humans: function and form. Function involves the many things that a dwelling must do for people, and you have identified basic functions. Form involves the physical characteristics which a dwelling must have to support necessary functions, and you have started thinking about the size of a dwelling as perhaps the most basic part of form. Congratulations! You're on the way to meeting the challenge.

As you progress through this chapter, you and your group may find that you will need to make modifications to your original plans. Don't be concerned about this, as this is typical of the planning and research process in which you are involved.

PHYSICS TO GO

1. a) Describe the weather in the area of the country in which you live.
   b) Describe some features of homes in your area that provide protection against the weather.

2. Choose another area of the country, or in the world, which has weather different from yours. Describe the weather in that area. Describe some features of homes in that area that provide protection against the weather.

3. A square foot (ft²) is a unit of measurement of surface area. Using a ruler, draw an accurate diagram of a square foot. (You may have to tape two pieces of paper together.) Label the dimensions of width and length.

4. Use your diagram of a square foot. Estimate the number of square feet in the room in which you are presently located.

5. a) Measure the length and width (in feet) of the room in which you are presently located.
   b) To calculate the area of a rectangle you multiply the length by the width.
      $A = l \times w$
      Calculate the area of the room you are in.
   c) How close was your estimate in question 4 to the area you calculated?

6. A family has decided to install a new floor in the kitchen of their home. The kitchen floor is a rectangle 8 feet wide and 12 feet long. The new floor will be covered with tiles which are square pieces measuring 1 foot on each side. How many tiles will be needed?

7. The family described in question 6 has changed its mind and has decided to use a type of flooring material that is available in square pieces measuring 2 feet on each side. How many pieces will be needed?

8. To prepare for Activity 2, determine the total floor area of your own or someone else's living spaces. Measure the amount of floor space in the bedrooms, the living areas, the kitchen, bathroom(s), and any other areas. Include any closets in your measurement. Place the data you collect on a 3×5 card, using the format shown here. All the information will be kept anonymous.

The Total Floor Area of a Home

Combined area of bedrooms in square feet: _____

Combined area of kitchens/eating areas in square feet: _____

Combined area of living room, den, etc. in square feet: _____

Total area of all the above spaces in square feet: _____

Combined area of bathroom(s) in your home in square feet: _____

Total areas of all other living spaces in square feet: _____

GRAND TOTAL of all living spaces in square feet: _____

The number of people occupying the space: _____

STRETCHING EXERCISE

Do a survey in your neighborhood. Make a list of, or draw features of homes that are well-suited to the local climate.

Activity Two

What is the "Right Size" for a Universal Dwelling?

WHAT DO YOU THINK?

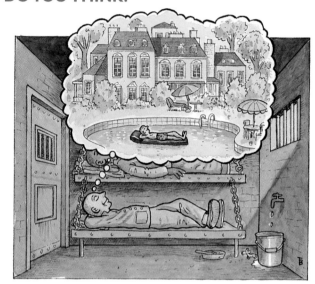

In some prisons in the United States, two inmates occupy an 8-foot by 10-foot cell. On the other hand, some people live in mansions of 10,000 to 20,000 square feet!

- **How much space do people need in their shelters to have a decent, humane life?**

Record your ideas about this question in your *Active Physics log*. Be prepared to discuss your responses with your small group and the class.

FOR YOU TO DO

1. Give the "Total Floor Area of a Home" index cards that you completed for today's class to your teacher. He or she will then read aloud the Grand Totals of the living spaces in square feet and the number of people who live in some of the homes.

   a) Enter these numbers in your log.

   b) Calculate the average number of square feet per person for at least five of the homes in your community.

2. Discuss the answers to the questions below with your group and then record the answers in your log.

a) How much total living space for all functions should your universal dwelling have per person?

b) Could you design a universal dwelling that would combine some living space functions? If so, how might you do this?

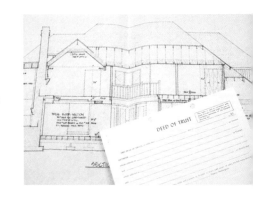

c) Will bathroom space be necessary for your universal dwelling? If not, explain how you might modify your dwelling if no indoor plumbing will be available. (Indoor plumbing is not available to many people in many countries.)

d) What size family (number of people) and what total square footage will you use for designing your "basic" universal dwelling? Explain your group's reasoning for choosing these family and dwelling sizes.

e) Decide on two additional sizes for your universal dwelling, the first to accommodate a larger family and the second to accommodate a smaller family. What will the square footage and family sizes of these versions be? What is your group's reasoning for deciding upon these specific larger and smaller sizes?

REFLECTING ON THE ACTIVITY AND THE CHALLENGE

Based upon the data that your class has collected, and your group discussions about what is needed in terms of living space for a universal dwelling, your group and other groups in the class have probably decided on universal dwellings of various sizes. This is another step toward completing the chapter challenge. You didn't just draw a size out of a hat. Your decision on size can be defended in terms of the data that you have collected about the sizes of homes of class members. You have also included necessary functions and various family sizes as factors in your decision.

There are probably a range of appropriate answers, but there is also opportunity to make changes and improvements as you proceed.

PHYSICS TO GO

1. Make a floor plan drawing of a room in your home, or someone else's home, or in your school. A floor plan drawing shows what the room looks like when viewed from above. It should show the shape of the room and the positions and sizes of the doors and windows. You will need a scale for your drawing, for example, one square on a sheet of graph paper could equal one square foot.

2. Make a vertical cross-section drawing of the same room you used in question 1. A vertical cross-section drawing should show what the room looks like when viewed from the side, including how high it is, and the shape and size of the windows and doors.

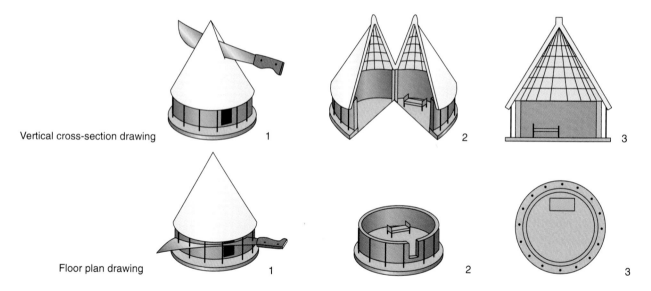

Vertical cross-section drawing   1   2   3

Floor plan drawing   1   2   3

How vertical cross-section and floor plan drawings are made.

3. A house lived in by an elderly man and woman has 1,500 square feet of floor area. Calculate the individual living space in square feet per person.

4. The house described in question 3 is sold to a young man and woman who have three children. Calculate the individual living space for the new family.

5. Here is a floor plan for houses being built for some people in Southern India.

   a) Calculate the number of square feet of living space the house has.
   b) If the average family size is 6 to 8 persons, what is the average living space per person?

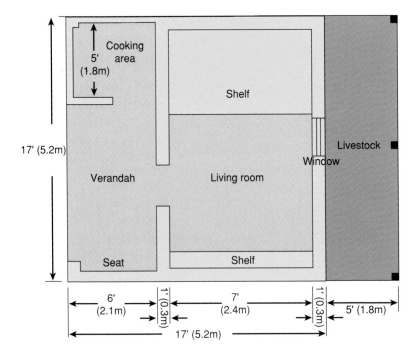

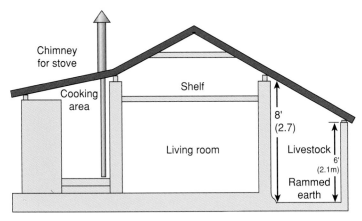

Typical family house—vertical cross-section drawing.

6. Look at the floor plan from Malawi of "a house that grows."
It allows the homeowner to add rooms to the house as the
household income or the family grow.

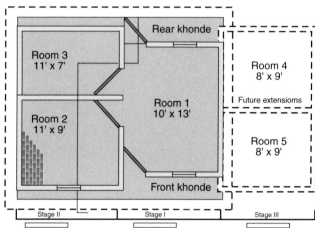

a) Calculate the number of square feet per person for a
newly married couple who builds Stage I (Room 1).

b) The couple has two children and decides to build Stage II
(Rooms 2 and 3). Calculate how may square feet there are
per person for this family of four.

c) The couple has two more children and then builds
Stage III (Rooms 4 and 5). Calculate the number of
square feet per person for this family of six.

7. Make a floor plan drawing and a vertical cross-section
drawing for your "universal" dwelling. Show the total square
footage of each room and the total square footage of the
dwelling. Include a scale for your drawing.

STRETCHING EXERCISES

1. Do research in your school library or on the Internet to find
information on the size of the "average American home."

2. Locate information on the amount of living space used by an
average person in another country.

Activity Three
The Shape of the "Universal Dwelling"

WHAT DO YOU THINK?

Throughout the world, homes take on many different shapes.

• **Why are most homes in the U.S. built in rectangular shapes?**

Record your ideas about this question in your *Active Physics log*. Be prepared to discuss your responses with your small group and the class.

FOR YOU TO DO

1. Make a closed 20-inch loop of string. You will also need pins and 1-inch square grid graph paper attached to a sheet of cardboard as shown on page H14.

2. Carefully place 4 pins at the intersections of grid lines. Run the closed loop of string around the pins. Adjust the pins until you have constructed a rectangle on your grid paper. The loop should form a tight fit around the perimeter.

   a) Count and record the number of one-inch squares that lie within this perimeter. Record your data in a table similar to the one shown on the following page.

HOME

Perimeter	Length of Long Sides	Length of Short Sides	Area Inside Perimeter

3. By carefully moving the pins, construct at least five more rectangles.

   a) Record the results in the table in your log.

4. Use the data you collected to help you answer the following questions.

   a) Which rectangle has the greatest perimeter, or do they all have equal perimeters?

   b) What happens to the area of the rectangle as one pair of sides gets longer while the perimeter stays the same?

   c) Which rectangle seems to have the largest internal area?

5. With your partner, use your loop of string and graph paper to determine how triangular (3-sided), pentagonal (5-sided), hexagonal (6-sided), octagonal (8-sided), and other shapes compare to that of a square of the same perimeter.

   a) Record your results in a table. (You can determine the area of the shapes by counting the number of boxes in the graph paper enclosed by the string. You will probably need to count half-boxes as well.)

   b) What appears to happen to the enclosed area as the number of sides increase?

   c) What shape do you think will generate the largest area for a given perimeter?

6. Extend your two-dimensional knowledge to three dimensions. Since homes are surrounded by walls and not string, you must consider how the information about enclosing the largest possible area with a loop of string can be used in designing your home.

   a) If you only had a limited quantity of material for walls to enclose a home, which shape would give the most living area? Why?

7. Meet with the other members of your group and, using the information you have gathered from these activities, choose a design shape for your universal dwelling. Your group will also have to determine the ceiling height, number of stories, and surface area-to-volume ratio for your basic dwelling design.

a) Record your group's decisions regarding these specifications in your log:

> The shape of the universal dwelling will be:
>
> The ceiling height of the rooms will be:
>
> The living space of the dwelling in square feet will be:
>
> The number of stories in the dwelling will be:
>
> The volume of the dwelling will be:

REFLECTING ON THE ACTIVITY AND THE CHALLENGE

Your group has reached some tentative decisions about how many square feet of living space per person your "universal dwelling" should have. You have to be concerned about making sure that you provide enough living space. You also need to make sure that the building is not too expensive to produce. This means that a good design will not require a large building to contain the floor space.

In this activity, you explored how you may construct a dwelling with the required floor space, while keeping the dimensions of the building small and the amount of materials needed to construct the building as small as possible.

Now you have addressed the two most basic questions about the form of the universal dwelling: size and shape. You can defend your choice of shape in terms of keeping the cost of materials low. You are on your way to being able to present your plan to the Architectural Committee with confidence.

PHYSICS TO GO

1. The total area of all the faces of an object is called the surface area. To calculate the total surface area, find the area of each of the faces, and then add these areas.

    To find the surface area of the following cube, you can imagine unfolding the cube to form a flat pattern.

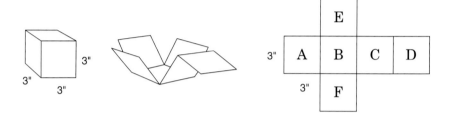

    a) What is the area of face A?
    b) What is the total surface area of the cube?

2. To find the surface area of the shape shown in the diagram below (a rectangular prism) you can once again imagine unfolding it to form a flat pattern.

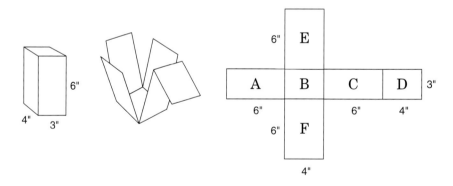

    a) Calculate the areas of A, B, C, D, E, and F.
    b) What is the surface area of the shape?

3. Find the surface areas of the following:

a)

4"
4"
4"

b)

5"
4"
2"

c)
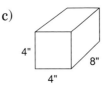
4"
8"
4"

4. To calculate the volume of a rectangular shape you can use the following relationship:

Volume = length × width × height

Calculate the volume of each figure in question 3.

5. Find the surface area-to-volume ratio of each figure in question 3. (Divide the surface area by its volume.) Which figure has the greatest surface area-to-volume ratio? the lowest?

6. A house was designed with outside walls that form a square base 27 feet on each side.

   a) Calculate the perimeter (distance around) of the house in feet.
   b) Calculate the total floor area of the house in square feet.

7. A house was designed with an outside wall that forms a circle which has a radius of 17.2 feet.

   a) Calculate the circumference of (distance around) the house in feet. The equation for the circumference of a circle is Circumference = 2 × π × radius.
      You can use a value of 3.14 for π.
   b) Calculate the total floor area of the house in square feet. The equation for the area of a circle is Area = π × radius × radius.

8. Use numbers to compare the houses in questions 6 and 7.

   a) If the height of the outside walls of the two houses were equal, how would the amount of paint needed to cover the walls compare? How significant is the difference?
   b) How do the total floor areas of the two houses compare? How significant is the difference?
   c) If living space of at least 180 square feet per person is needed, how many persons could live in each house? How significant is this difference?

9. A research outpost for a scientist in a remote part of Alaska has a hut shelter which is a cube 8 feet on each side. The scientist sometimes visits a nearby family who lives in a two-story cabin also shaped as a cube. The cabin's dimensions are double the dimensions of the hut, measuring 16 feet on each side. Use the numbers to make the following comparisons:

   a) Compare the total floor areas of the two dwellings as a ratio. (The cabin has an upstairs level.)
   b) Compare the outside surface areas of the two dwellings including the bottom floor of each. Express the comparison as a ratio.
   c) Compare the volumes of the two dwellings as a ratio.
   d) Calculate the surface area-to-volume ratio for each dwelling. (Divide the outside surface area of each dwelling by its volume. The answers will be in units of square feet per cubic foot.) Which dwelling has the greatest possibility for heat loss through its surfaces per cubic foot of inside volume?

10. Using the information you gathered in this activity, modify your floor plan drawing and section drawing for your "universal" dwelling. Show the total square footage of each room and the total square footage of the dwelling. Include a scale for your drawing.

Activity Four

Solar Heat Flow in the "Universal Dwelling"

WHAT DO YOU THINK?

Throughout one cloudless day in June, at 45° North latitude, over 300 million joules of solar radiation strike each square meter of area at the Earth's surface.

• **What is the relationship between how fast a building heats and how fast it cools? (Do buildings that heat quickly, cool slowly; or do buildings that heat quickly, cool quickly?)**

Record your ideas about these questions in your *Active Physics log*. Be prepared to discuss your responses with your small group and the class.

FOR YOU TO DO

1. Using the resources that have been provided, construct a scale model of your universal dwelling using the design specifications for the basic unit. The model home should be built on a scale of 1:48. That means that one inch on the model will equal four feet, or 48", on the real home. In order to build the model quickly, build only the walls and roof of your home. Don't worry about putting a bottom (floor) on the model or placing windows and doors at this time.

2. Using the figure below, assemble a heat lamp, ring stand support and clamp, timer, measuring tools and thermometers. Conduct a timed heat-transfer experiment of 20 min. Place the nearest edge of the model 20 cm from the bulb of the heat lamp, with the lamp at approximately 45° from the center of the model home. (A 45° angle is halfway between the vertical and the horizontal.)

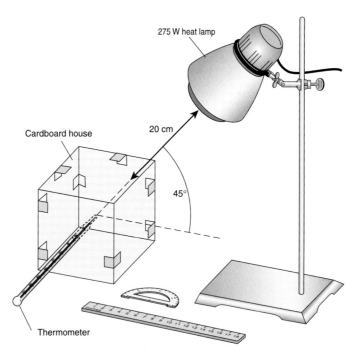

275 W heat lamp

Cardboard house

20 cm

45°

Thermometer

If the thermometer should break, _immediately_ notify your instructor.

3. Carefully make a small hole in one wall. After making the hole, place the thermometer (or temperature probe) into one side of your model so that the bulb or probe is located in the dead center of the model. Be sure you can read the thermometer once it is in place!

4. When you have your model, the thermometer, and the heat
   lamp placed properly, have your teacher check it before you
   begin heating.

⚠ **Caution: Heat lamps get very hot. Be careful not to touch the bulb or housing surrounding the bulb.**

   🖎 a) Record the temperature of the thermometer before heating
      and record this as the temperature at 0 time.
   🖎 b) Turn on the heat lamp and, after 30 s, record the
      temperature.
   🖎 c) Continue this procedure for 10 min, recording
      temperature at each 30-s interval.

5. Turn off the lamp at the end of the 10-min heating phase.

   🖎 a) Continue to record the temperature every minute after the
      lamp is turned off for another 10 min.
   🖎 b) Calculate and record the change in temperature during
      each timed interval of heating and cooling.
   🖎 c) Graph your recorded data (temperatures against time) on
      the graph paper provided by your teacher. Your time axis
      should extend from 0 min (when you began) to
      20 min (after the experiment was completed), and be
      placed on the *x*-axis.

6. Use the graph and the data you recorded to answer the
   following questions.

   🖎 a) What was the total temperature increase in your model
      home during the heating phase?
   🖎 b) What was the total temperature decrease in your model
      home during the cooling phase?
   🖎 c) Was the rate of temperature increase constant? How do
      you know?
   🖎 d) Was the rate of temperature decrease constant? How do
      you know?
   🖎 e) What time of day did the heating phase represent?
   🖎 f) What time of day did the cooling phase represent?
   🖎 g) What does your experiment suggest in regard to the
      potential of your model home to be heated by solar
      energy?

REFLECTING ON THE ACTIVITY AND THE CHALLENGE

Over the past three activities you have made good progress in deciding upon the design specifications for your universal dwelling. In the last activity, you explored finding the "best fit" between living space and minimum surface area for your universal dwelling.

There are several reasons why you would want to keep surface area of the dwelling small, while keeping the interior as large as possible. One reason is that the materials for construction of the surface area of a building are expensive and a smaller surface area requires fewer materials. Another reason has to do with controlling the inside temperature of the building. In this activity, you constructed a model of your universal dwelling and investigated its heating and cooling properties.

The Architectural Committee probably will have some hard questions for you about your plans for heating and cooling the dwelling you are designing. That's because the greatest cost in operating most homes is for heating and cooling the home. This activity has given you some baseline information about how your dwelling design responds to the best kind of energy: free energy from the sun. It will be important for you to learn how to use solar energy to best advantage in the next activities. You do not want to design a building that is expensive to heat or cool.

PHYSICS TO GO

1. If four feet of length on a real home is represented by one inch on a scale model of the home, what length on the scale model would represent one foot on the real home?

2. A 1:48 scale drawing of the floor plan of a home must fit one $8\frac{1}{2} \times 11$ inch sheet of paper. What maximum length and width in feet can the home have?

3. Home designers sometimes use a 1:96 scale ($\frac{1}{8}$ inch represents 1 foot) when making drawings of home plans. What advantages would a 1:96 scale have over a 1:48 scale ($\frac{1}{4}$ inch represents 1 foot)?

4. If the heat lamp represented the sun at its noon position during the heating phase of the activity, which side of the model dwelling–north, south, east, or west–must have been facing the sun?

5. Describe how you would need to change the position of the heat lamp relative to the model dwelling to have the lamp represent the sun during the morning or afternoon.

6. Do you think that all of the radiation from the heat lamp that hit the model dwelling was absorbed by the dwelling? Give evidence to support your answer.

7. Explain how you think heat travelled from the inside surface of the model dwelling to the thermometer at the center of the model during the heating phase. Obviously, the heat had to travel through the air inside the model. How did it do that?

STRETCHING EXERCISE

1. Write down three questions that you would ask someone who uses solar heating or solar cooling for their home.

2. If you know of any people who use solar energy to heat their homes, or have designed ways to keep solar energy out to keep their homes cool, you may wish to talk with them about how they have done this. Ask them about the special things that they have done to control the effects of solar energy on their homes.

Activity Five

The Role of Insulation: Investigating Insulation Types

WHAT DO YOU THINK?

Insulation used in homes is usually a lightweight material that is designed to reduce the flow of heat energy through the walls or ceiling.

- **Is insulation in a home more important in the heat of summer or the cool of winter?**

Record your ideas about this question in your *Active Physics log*. Be prepared to discuss your responses with your small group and the class.

FOR YOU TO DO

1. Place the insulating material supplied to your team in each of the 3 cans. Insert a thermometer in the absolute center of each material.

   🖎 a) Measure the thickness of the insulation surrounding the thermometer in each can.

   🖎 b) Record the temperature shown by each thermometer.

2. Place the 3 cans in a hot water bath.

   🖎 a) Record the temperature of each can every minute for 10 min.

⚠ **Do not change the temperature setting on the hot water bath.**

3. Carefully check that the cans are not too hot to touch. Carefully remove the cans from the bath.

   🖎 a) Record the temperature each minute for another 10 min.

⚠ **Use a cloth or paper towel to grasp the cans when removing them from the baths. Moisture may form on the outside—be careful that the can does not slip from your grasp.**

4. Now place the 3 cans in an ice water bath and repeat the steps above.

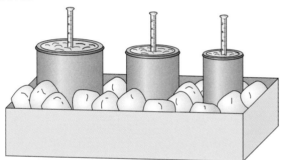

   🖎 a) Record the temperature in each can every minute for 10 min of cooling in the bath and for another 10 min after removing them from the bath.

⚠ **If the thermometer should break, *immediately* notify your instructor.**

5. Display the data on a graph.

   🖎 a) Graph your heating and cooling data for each of the 3 cans on a single graph, labeling each appropriately.

6. Use your graph to answer the following questions:

   🖎 a) Compare the three graphs that you made. What differences do you note among the graphs?

   🖎 b) What do you conclude about the effectiveness of insulation in heating as opposed to cooling situations?

   🖎 c) What do you conclude about the effectiveness of using varying thickness of insulating material?

FOR YOU TO READ

Transmission of Heat Energy

You have most likely studied in prior science classes the three means by which heat energy is transmitted: conduction, convection, and radiation. As you read the descriptions of these means of transmission, try to recall experiments or investigations that you pursued if you studied this earlier.

In the case of conduction, the heat energy possessed by a material is transmitted to another material by direct contact of the materials with one another. The rapidly moving (and hence high energy) atoms in a red hot iron bar come in direct contact with, let us say, cold water. The heat energy of the iron atoms is conducted by physical contact directly to the water molecules, which, in turn, heat other adjacent molecules and so on, causing the heat energy to dissipate throughout the water, warming it in the process.

In convection, the molecules or atoms of a fluid (a liquid or a gas) which have more heat energy will move faster than the surrounding molecules of that material. As a result, they will move further apart and, therefore, become pushed by the colder, more closely packed molecules or atoms. As the hotter, lower-density molecules move through the colder surrounding material, they carry their heat energy (motion) with them, losing it along their path to other colder molecules by conduction. Convection then, is the transmission of heat energy from one place to another due to physical movement of a warmer fluid through a colder fluid (typically in response to the force of gravity).

Radiation is the third form of energy transmission. In this case, the electromagnetic radiation given off by high energy (hot) materials can be transmitted through objects, or even a vacuum, at the speed of light. When this energy strikes a material that can absorb it, the radiant energy causes the atoms or molecules of the material it strikes to move faster and the molecules now have more heat energy.

REFLECTING ON THE ACTIVITY AND THE CHALLENGE

Homes For Everyone (HFE) realizes that it is important to control the interior temperatures of their universal dwellings regardless of climate and location. It is important because of energy, comfort, and health concerns.

One of the criteria that the Architectural Committee will use to evaluate your plan is "the kind of insulation materials and thickness you choose should show you know the principles which make the insulation effective." That's exactly what this activity was about, so it will be very helpful in meeting the challenge.

PHYSICS TO GO

1. Explain how conduction, convection, and radiation were involved in both the heating and cooling phases of the model dwelling in Activity Four.

2. Which of the three ways of transferring heat was most directly involved in the investigation in Activity Five? Explain your answer.

3. In this activity you tested the effects of two variables on the transfer of heat. Identify the variables and explain what you learned about the effect of each on heat transfer.

4. If you wanted to reduce the amount of heat conducted through a particular kind of material to one-half the amount, what change in the thickness of the material would be needed? Also provide answers for reducing the transfer of heat to one-third, and one-fourth the amount.

5. Would insulating a home be more, less, or about equally important for keeping a home warm in a cold climate or keeping a home cool in a hot climate? Use evidence from the data for your answer.

6. Years ago, the answer to keeping warm during cold weather was to put on more clothes. Today, the answer can be to put on different clothes. Comment on these two ways of keeping warm in terms of the variables tested in this activity, and the evolution of clothing available for winter.

7. Find out what kinds and thickness of insulating materials are used in the walls and ceiling of your home. Your parents or building supervisor may have this information.

8. Go to a building supply store and examine various insulating materials. The insulating properties of these materials are given in "R values." Find out what an "R value" is.

9. Some rigid insulating material has an aluminum foil surface bonded to the sheet. What purpose does this aluminum foil surface serve? How does it influence the "R value" of the material?

10. How much insulation is recommended for a home in your area of the country?

11. Is the amount of insulation recommended the same for floors, walls, and ceilings? Why?

STRETCHING EXERCISE

Design a beverage container to keep a cold drink cold, and a hot drink hot.

INQUIRY INVESTIGATION

Design an experiment to test the insulating effectiveness of natural material such as grass, dry mud, adobe brick, or stone. After your teacher approves your design, conduct the experiment.

Activity Six

Investigating Insulation Placement in Your Universal Dwelling

WHAT DO YOU THINK?

The density (mass per unit volume) of air decreases with temperature, leading to the common knowledge expression, "heat rises."

- **Why are attics of homes so hot on a summer day?**
- **What are these same attics like on a cold winter day?**

Record your ideas about these questions in your *Active Physics log*. Be prepared to discuss your responses with your small group and the class.

FOR YOU TO DO

1. Cut the cardboard as insulation so that it will fit snugly within the ceiling of your model home. Use masking tape to fix it in place.

2. Set up your experiment in the same manner as you did for Activity 4. Be sure to keep the lamp at the same distance (20 cm) and at the same 45° angle as in the first experiment.

   a) Construct a temperature vs. time graph of your data as you did in Activity 4.

   b) Compare this heat transfer experiment data with data from Activity 4 and interpret the results.

   c) How did insulating the ceiling affect the heating and cooling of your model?

3. Insulate the walls of your model in the same way as you did the ceiling. Repeat the heat transfer experiment.

   a) Compare and interpret these results with the first two experiments.

4. Use the results of Activities 4 and 6 to answer the following questions.

   a) Compare the results of your team's findings with those of the other teams.

   b) How do you explain the similarities and differences?

   c) Given the scale of your model home, to what thickness of insulation in a real home does your $\frac{1}{4}$ inch of cardboard insulation correspond?

   d) What effect do you predict would occur if you used twice the thickness of cardboard in your model? Three times the thickness? Defend your response with data from Activity 5.

REFLECTING ON THE ACTIVITY AND THE CHALLENGE

In this activity, you insulated your model home and then tested it to see what effects insulating will have on controlling the internal temperature of the home. The Architectural Committee will expect you to be able to show that you know where insulation is most effective in trapping energy. You now have gathered scientific data which you can use to show that you know where to place insulation most effectively in a home.

PHYSICS TO GO

1. In insulating a real home you probably wouldn't use cardboard as the insulating material as you did for the model dwelling. What materials might you use, and why?

2. What considerations, other than the effect of the insulation, might guide your choices of insulating materials for a home? Think about fire prevention.

3. Homes are usually designed to have about twice as much insulating effect in ceilings than in exterior walls. Why?

4. Could a vacuum be a good insulator? Explain why or why not, and under what conditions.

5. Compare and contrast the purpose of insulation in hot weather versus cold weather. Should placement of insulation be different for these different purposes?

6. Insulating materials for homes are rated on a relative scale of "R" values. Sheets or rolls of different kinds of materials in various thickness are available, and each has an assigned R value. The R values of two or more thickness can be added together to find the total insulating value of combined layers. What combinations of the following materials could be used to provide R-19 insulation for a wall and R-38 insulation for a ceiling?

   - R-8 expanded polystyrene board 2 inches thick
   - R-11 fiberglass wool $3\frac{1}{2}$ inches thick
   - R-30 fiberglass wool $9\frac{1}{2}$ inches thick

7. In preparation for tomorrow's class work, collect the following information tonight at your home.

   a) Measure all the windows in your home and calculate the total number of square feet of window area of your home. Record your calculation.

   b) Measure all the exterior wall surface areas of your home, and calculate the total number of square feet (including the window areas) of exterior walls of your home. Record your calculation.

   c) Divide the total window area by the total wall surface area. Record your calculation.

STRETCHING EXERCISES

1. In constructing homes today, high, open (cathedral) ceilings are often part of the design plans for the living space. What advantages and disadvantages do high ceilings have with respect to heating and cooling considerations for the home?

2. Contemporary homes in America today are built with full basements, half buried basements, or are constructed on top of concrete slabs cast on the surface. What heating advantages and disadvantages do you believe would exist for each of these types of house foundation? Explain your responses for each type of foundation.

Activity Seven

The Role of Windows...Placing Windows in Your Universal Dwelling

WHAT DO YOU THINK?

It is often said, "A window hasn't been made that is as good as a well-insulated wall."

- **Should all sides of the model dwelling have the same area of windows? Why or why not?**

Record your ideas about these questions in your *Active Physics log*. Be prepared to discuss your responses with your small group and the class.

FOR YOU TO DO

1. Compile a chart in your group to summarize your calculations of window area to wall area ratios in your homes.

   ✎ a) What is the average window to wall area ratio for your group?

2. Use all the information and resources available to you. Decide upon the number, sizes, and placement of the windows for your model home. Remember, you want to provide for optimal lighting and ventilation and you also want to allow solar energy to enter the home and heat it when needed. However, you do not want to transfer large amounts of energy from the home to the outside when direct sunlight does not enter the window.

   ✎ a) Approximate the window to wall area ratio you plan to use in your model home.

   ✎ b) How does the window to wall area ratio for your model home compare to the average window to wall area ratio you calculated for your group? Explain why you chose the ratio you did.

3. Draw outlines of the windows to scale on the walls of your model and carefully cut out the windows with a cutting tool.

4. Use masking tape to tape transparent food wrap over the window cutouts.

5. Repeat the heat transfer experiment with the heat lamp on your model home. Place the heat lamp and model home so that the lamp is shining on the home at the same angle and at the same distance as in previous activities.

   ✎ a) Record and graph your findings as you did in previous activities.

   ✎ b) Compare your heating and cooling graphs for this activity with those in Activities Four and Six. How do the graphs differ? Explain your results.

⚠ **Caution: The cutting tools are very sharp. Be careful and get help from your teacher as needed.**

REFLECTING ON THE ACTIVITY
AND THE CHALLENGE

Virtually all dwellings have windows of one type or another to provide interior light and to provide for ventilation and temperature control. The windows in a home built today are extremely well-designed and engineered in comparison to those of 30 years ago. The problem your group faces is a complicated one. You wish to design and place windows in your Homes For Everyone (HFE) universal dwelling to provide for optimal lighting and ventilation, but you also know that windows have energy advantages and disadvantages. Windows, which can allow solar energy to enter the home and heat it when needed, lose heat through conduction, convection, and radiation to a much greater degree than the insulated walls.

You will need to convince the Architectural Committee that you understand that windows offer both advantages and disadvantages. You have gathered evidence by comparing the heating and cooling curves from this activity to the corresponding curves from Activity Six.

PHYSICS TO GO

1. Heat can enter and leave a home through windows. How are conduction, convection, and radiation involved in

   a) the transfer of heat into a home through its windows?
   b) the transfer of heat out of a home through its windows?

2. The amount of heat gained or lost through a window is directly proportional to the surface area of the window.

   a) Compare the amount of heat expected to be transferred through a window 2 feet wide by 2 feet high to the amount expected for a window 4 feet wide by 4 feet high.
   b) Glass doors behave about the same as windows regarding heat transfer. Compare the amount of heat expected to be transferred through a glass patio door 8 feet wide by 6 feet high to the amount expected for a 2 feet by 2 feet window.

3. Visit a building supply store in your community. Examine the windows available. Find out about the following:

a) The R value of the cheapest and most expensive windows.
b) The difference between thermopane and single pane windows.
c) Why thermopane windows are built the way they are.
d) What "low E" windows are, and how they function.

4. Even the highest quality windows do not have as much insulating effect as a well insulated wall. Explain why.

5. Window drapes and shades can provide privacy and beauty in a home. Explain how they may also be used to control heat transfer through windows.

6. Designs for energy-efficient homes in parts of the U.S. that have cold winters have very few if any windows on the north side of the home. Why?

7. People who live in warm climates often use air conditioners to cool their homes. What if any problems do windows present related to air conditioners?

STRETCHING EXERCISES

Find out about passive solar heating for homes. Answer the following:

a) How can adding more windows to a house serve to warm the house during the day?

b) How can you prevent heat from escaping from these extra windows during the night?

c) What can be used to store the heat that is collected during the day?

d) Where should windows for passive solar heating be placed to be most effective?

Activity Eight
Investigating Overhangs and Awnings

WHAT DO YOU THINK?

Heating and air conditioning are the most expensive items for operating the average American home.

- **What can be done so that windows will let sun enter the dwelling when it is cold outside, and block sunlight from entering when it is hot outside?**

Record your ideas about these questions in your *Active Physics log*. Be prepared to discuss your responses with your small group and the class.

FOR YOU TO DO

1. Find the latitude of the location for which you are designing your model home.

2. In the temperate regions, the sun is low in the sky at noon in winter and high in the sky at noon in summer. In fact, it is this changing elevation of the sun which causes the winter and summer temperature differences.

a) Use the example below and the figure to the left to help you calculate the angle of the sun at noon at the winter and summer solstices in your area.

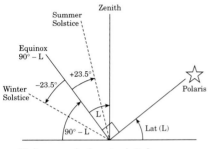

Finding sun angles for a given latitude

Example:
The latitude of St. Louis, Missouri, is 38 degrees North. Calculate the noon altitude of the sun as viewed from St. Louis on the equinoxes and solstices.

Sun angle on equinoxes = (90 degrees) minus (latitude angle)
$$= 90° - 38°$$
$$= 52°$$

Sun angle on summer solstice = (Sun angle on equinoxes) plus (23.5°)
$$= 52° + 23.5°$$
$$= 75.5°$$

Sun angle on winter solstice = (Sun angle on equinoxes) minus (23.5)
$$= 52° - 23.5°$$
$$= 28.5°$$

b) Use the same figure and example to help you calculate the angle of the sun at noon at the winter and summer soltices in the area for which you are designing a model home.

3. Set up your model home and the heat lamp as in previous activities.

4. Use a protractor and the sun angle data to adjust the heat lamp so that it matches the angle position of the sun at noon at the summer solstice.

a) Measure, record, and graph the heating and cooling curves for your model home.

5. With the lamp turned on, place a small piece of tag board over one of the windows on the side of the model facing the heat lamp. Try different widths of tag board and the angles of attachment until you find the width and/or angle that will entirely block the lamp's light but still provide someone inside with a view. Use masking tape to attach tag board awnings and/or roof overhangs to your model.

6. Repeat the heat transfer experiment on your model home that is now fitted with awnings or overhangs for summer solstice conditions.

✎ a) Record and graph your data.

7. Do not change the awnings or overhangs on your model, but adjust the lamp so its position matches the angle of the sun at the winter solstice. Repeat the heat transfer experiment.

✎ a) Record and graph this data on the same graph.

✎ b) What differences do you note in the summer and winter solstice heating graphs? How do you explain the differences?

REFLECTING ON THE ACTIVITY AND THE CHALLENGE

One of the main requirements is that the universal dwelling must be able to be used in a wide variety of locations on Earth. Since the dwelling also depends on energy from the sun, you must include in your design the knowledge about how solar energy varies with location on the Earth. This activity has prepared you to answer questions which the Architectural Committee will ask about how your design allows for solar energy at different locations.

PHYSICS TO GO

1. Imagine yourself standing outdoors at noon at your home latitude. You are facing straight South toward the horizon. You are doing this on four special days during the year whose titles are listed below. For each special day give its date, explain its meaning in terms of seasons, and then predict the angle of the sun above the horizon.

a) Vernal equinox   b) Summer solstice

c) Autumnal equinox   d) Winter solstice

2. Latitudes in the continental U.S. vary from about 25° North to 50° North. Calculate the angle of the sun above the South horizon on the summer solstice for the latitudes listed below:

   a) 25° North
   b) 30° North
   c) 35° North
   d) 40° North
   e) 45° North

3. One town in the U.S. is 2,000 miles west of another town. At noon on the winter solstice at each town, the sun is observed to have an altitude of 26°. What is the latitude of each town?

4. The latitude of Mexico City, Mexico is 19° North. Do a calculation to show yourself that the sun will shine on the north side of a home in Mexico City at noon on the summer solstice. State a rule for locations in Earth's northern hemisphere where this can happen.

5. Sketch a design for a roof overhang or window awning that will always shade a south-facing window from the noontime sun during the six months between the vernal and autumnal equinoxes, but will allow the noon sun to shine on the entire window during the other six months of the year.

6. The sun shines on windows on the east and west sides of a home, too, but for only part of the day. What could be done to control heat gains and losses through those windows?

7. Do you think the added cost of building a roof overhang or using awnings on your model dwelling would be worth the additional expense? Why or why not?

8. Shades are more effective than awnings for blocking sun from entering windows on the east and west sides of buildings. Why is this so?

PHYSICS AT WORK

Ray Aguilera

HABITAT FOR HUMANITY

Ray is the construction manager at the Valley in the Sun, Arizona, Habitat for Humanity branch. Habitat for Humanity International is a non-profit organization that seeks to eliminate poverty, housing, and homelessness from the world. They do this by building and selling homes for no profit, to families who cannot get conventional financing. Homeowners also become partners in the process by contributing 500 hours of "sweat equity" toward the construction of their own home.

Our former President, Jimmy Carter, has been deeply committed to Habitat since 1984. Each year former President Carter and his wife, Rosalynn, join Habitat volunteers to build homes and raise awareness of the critical need for affordable housing.

Ray Aguilera was on his way to becoming a lawyer, when one summer he got a job building homes, and has never stopped. Ray gets a great deal of satisfaction from his work with Habitat. "I enjoy going from an empty lot and watching something magical grow out of it," he says.

Arizona has a different climate than many other places in the country and takes special considerations when planning homes. In this Southwestern desert, the temperatures are often in the 100s and rarely very cold. For example, the foundations and footings for houses do not need as much concrete as other places because the soil conditions are so different. And, in Arizona, you never have to worry about winter frosts. "The most essential characteristic of building a house in Arizona," states Ray, "is to keep it energy efficient. We also strive to design houses that will blend in with the existing environment. In Arizona, we make more of an effort to keep the hot out and the cold in. To do this we use double-paned windows, and as much insulation as we can fit between the walls and in the attic."

Chapter 1 Assessment Physics You Learned

You and your group have been investigating the design of your model universal dwelling for this entire chapter. You have learned a great deal about this problem and have explored possible solutions. You now have reached the point where you must finalize your plans and prepare your presentation for the hearing before the HFE Architectural Committee. Good luck!

Using the resources that you have been provided with, develop scale drawings of your model universal dwelling. Refer back to the challenge given at the beginning of this chapter to guide your group's activities. Your presentations will be strictly limited to five minutes, so make every drawing and sentence count!

Review the criteria you decided the HFE Architectural Committee should use in evaluating your drawings and your written presentation.

Surface area-to-volume ratio

Brief statements of conduction, convection, radiation

Heating curves and Cooling curves
> With opaque backgrounds
> With windows
> With insulation
> With awnings

Properties of insulation

Effect of thickness on insulation effectiveness

Brief review of latitude and solar position at equinox

ELECTRICITY FOR EVERYONE

CHAPTER 2

Throughout history people have tried to help other people. However, changes often have been made without any respect for the personal and cultural needs of those who are being assisted.

If you ever become involved in a self-help community group, it would be important for you to work together with the people you are helping in assessing their needs, and their capabilities. Although that is not possible given your limited time in class, you should recognize the need for this type of collaborative teamwork when assisting people.

Scenario

The Homes For Everyone (HFE) Architectural Committee has just accepted your design for a "universal" dwelling to meet the growing housing shortage in many diverse areas of the world. The organization would now like you to develop an appliance package that would help meet the basic needs for healthy, enjoyable living for the families who will reside in the universal dwellings.

The source of electrical energy chosen for this particular project is a wind generator. The following is a description of the wind-generator system chosen for HFE. Try to get a sense of the meaning of unfamiliar words. When the chapter is completed, you will understand these terms.

The wind-generator system chosen for HFE is a highly reliable, mass-produced model that has an output of 2400 W (2.4 kW). Experience has shown that in areas having only moderate average wind speed (6 to 8 km/h) the generator system will deliver a monthly energy output of about 90 kWh (kilowatt-hours) to the home, or about 3 kWh per day.

Direct current (DC) from the wind-driven generator is stored in batteries that allow storage of electrical energy to keep the home going for four windless days. The batteries deliver DC electricity, but most home appliances are designed to use alternating current (AC). An inverter changes the DC from the batteries into AC before it enters the home. A circuit breaker rated at 2400 W protects the batteries from overheating if too much energy is asked for at any single time. Finally, a kiloWatt-hour meter is provided to keep track of the amount of electrical energy that has been used. The result is that the dwelling will have the same kind of electricity delivered to it as do most homes in the U.S., but less electrical power and energy will be available than for the average homes in the U.S.

Challenge

You will use your experience with electricity in your home and what you learn in this chapter to decide which electrical appliances, powered by a wind generator, can and should be provided for the HFE dwellings.

1. Your first task is to decide what electrical appliances can and should be used to meet the basic needs of the people whose HFE dwelling will be served by a wind generator.

- **Use the list of appliances on pages H72 - H73, any additional information that you can gather about appliances, and the characteristics of the wind-generator system to decide what appliances to include in an "appliance package" for HFE.**

- **As part of your decision-making process, determine if it seems best to provide a basic appliance package that would be the same for all dwellings, or if packages should be adapted with "options" to allow for factors such as different family sizes, climates, or other local conditions.**

- **Describe how each appliance in your package will contribute to the well-being of the people who live in the dwelling.**

2. Your second task is educational. The people will need to be instructed how to stay within the power and energy limits of their electrical system as they use their appliances.

- **You must outline a training manual for volunteers who will be going into the field to teach the inhabitants about the HFE wind-generator system and the appliances. The volunteers have no special knowledge of electricity. Therefore, the volunteers need a "crash course" that will prepare**
them to teach the people to use their electrical system with success.

- **Two factors will be especially important to teach: the power demand of the combination of appliances being used at any one time may not exceed 2400 W, and the average daily total consumption of electrical energy should not exceed 3 kWh.**

Criteria

The criteria for this challenge will be judged on the basis of 100 points. Discuss the criteria below, add details to the criteria if it would be helpful, and agree as a class on the point allocation.

- **The list of appliances to be included in the HFE appliance package must be as comprehensive as possible, and it must be clear how each appliance will enhance the health or well-being of the people who live in the dwelling.**

- **The outline of the training manual for HFE volunteers must explain the difference between 2400 W and 3 kWh. It must also give clear examples of how use of the appliances in the package can be scheduled to stay within the power and energy limits of the electrical system on both a daily and a long-term basis.**

Activity One
Generate

WHAT DO YOU THINK?

Electricity affects most parts of your life. You pay for it, over and over, in the form of electric bills and batteries. Also, most products that you purchase are manufactured by processes that use electricity, so you pay for electricity in indirect ways, too.

• **Is there any "free" electricity available and, if so, why pay for it?**

Record your ideas about this question in your *Active Physics log*. Be prepared to discuss your responses with your small group and the class.

FOR YOU TO DO

1. You will be provided with a bulb, bulb base, connecting wires and a generator. Assemble the bulb, bulb base, connecting wires, and hand generator, and turn the crank of the generator to make the bulb light. Never turn the crank too fast. You can strip the gears!

   a) Draw a diagram of how you assembled the equipment for the bulb to light.

   b) Under what conditions will the bulb not light? Use words and a diagram in your answer.

   c) What are the effects of changing the speed or direction of cranking the generator?

   d) What are the effects of reversing the connections of the wires to the bulb or to the generator?

2. Replace the bulb that you have been using with a blinking bulb, the kind used in some toys, flashlights, and decorations. As before, use the generator to make it light, and keep cranking the generator to make the bulb go through several on and off cycles.

   a) Describe any difference that you can feel in cranking the generator when the bulb is on compared to when the bulb is off.

   b) How do you think that the blinking bulb works? What makes it go on and off?

3. Replace the blinking bulb with a strand of steel wool within the bulb socket. Crank the generator and observe what happens to the steel wool. Be careful not to touch the hot steel wool! You may push the steel wool with the point of a pencil to provide a better contact with the socket.

   a) Describe the appearance of the steel wool.

   b) What factors affect whether or not the steel wool glows, how much it glows, and for how long?

   c) What were the similarities and differences between the steel wool and the light bulbs as used above?

The steel wool will get very hot. Do not touch it while conducting the experiment. Allow it to cool before removing it.

4. Was the electrical energy that you used to "light things up" in this activity "free"? Did you get something for nothing? Using your observations in this activity, write a short paragraph to answer each of the following questions.

a) What was the energy source for each part of the activity (bulb, blinking bulb, steel wool)? Was it free energy, at no cost?

b) What forms of energy were involved in the activity, and in what order did the forms appear?

c) How is the energy source used in this activity different from the source used to light a bulb in a flashlight, or in a house lamp?

REFLECTING ON THE ACTIVITY AND THE CHALLENGE

This activity has given you some experience with a process that is involved in the electrical system you will use for the HFE dwelling: using a generator to provide energy for electric light bulbs. The generator and the light bulbs used in this activity are scaled-down versions of the ones to be used for the dwelling, but they work in the same way. One additional feature will exist in the electrical system for the dwelling, the electrical energy from the generator will be able to be stored in batteries until it is needed to operate lights and other appliances.

Part of your challenge is to write a training manual to help instructors teach the inhabitants about their wind-generator system. You will probably want to include what you learned in this activity in your manual.

PHYSICS TO GO

1. Make a chart with two columns, the first one labelled "Word" and the other labelled "Meaning."

a) In the first column make a list of "electricity words"— words that you have heard used in connection with electrical units of measurement, parts of electrical systems, or how electricity behaves.

b) In the second column write what *you* think each word means, or describes.

2. You know that electricity comes "out of the wall." You also know that it "starts" in a power plant. Draw a picture that shows how *you* think the electricity is "created" and how it gets to your home.

3. Explain what *you* think electricity is, how it behaves, and how it does what it does.

4. A variety of energy sources are used to operate light bulbs. Identify as many energy sources as you can which are used to power light sources.

5. The kind of light bulb you used in this activity is called "incandescent." Another kind of light bulb often used is called "fluorescent." Look up the meaning of the two words and explain how they are related to what glows to cause each kind of bulb to give off light.

6. "You don't get something for nothing." Explain how this expression applies to using a hand-operated generator to light a bulb.

STRETCHING EXERCISES

Some light bulbs are frosted on the inside, while others are clear. Some light bulbs have built-in reflectors to make them serve as a spotlight or a floodlight. Research different types of light bulbs. On a poster, describe how each is different, how each works, and where and why each is useful.

HOME

Activity Two
Lighten Up

WHAT DO YOU THINK?

Lights were the first electric appliances for homes.

- **How do light bulbs, and the electricity that makes them glow, work?**

Record your ideas about this question in your *Active Physics log*. Be prepared to discuss your responses with your small group and the class.

FOR YOU TO DO

1. Before you begin this activity, remind yourself about the "feel" of the generator and the brightness of the bulb when the generator was used to energize one bulb in Activity 1. Connect a single bulb to the generator and crank. Use your observations of a single bulb as a basis for comparison when you use two or more bulbs during this activity.

2. There are two distinct ways to connect more than one light bulb to the generator. Look at the two diagrams showing three bulbs connected in **series** and in **parallel.**

✎ a) Describe in your log how the two circuits are different.

✎ b) Make predictions about how each circuit operates.

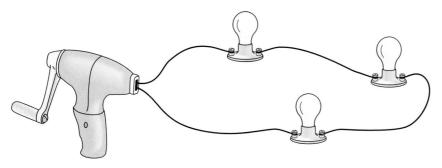

A series circuit.

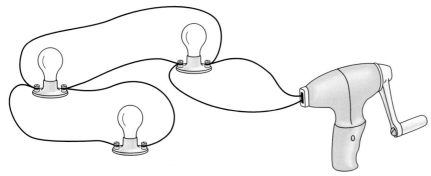

A parallel circuit.

3. Connect *two* bulbs in series with the generator. Use the diagram showing three bulbs connected in series to help you. Crank the generator, and notice the "feel" of the generator and the brightness of the bulbs. Repeat this for three bulbs, and four bulbs.

✎ a) Describe what happens and try to explain why it happens.

4. What would happen if, in a series circuit of several bulbs, one bulb were to be disconnected, or burn out? Try it by unscrewing one bulb from its base while the circuit is operating.

✎ a) Describe what happens, and try to explain why it happens.

5. Connect *two* bulbs in parallel with the generator, and, again, observe the "feel" of the generator and the brightness of the bulbs. Repeat this for three bulbs, and four bulbs.

✎a) Describe your observations and compare them to your predictions for a parallel circuit.

6. What would happen if one bulb were to fail in a parallel circuit? Try it by unscrewing one bulb.

✎a) Describe what happens, and try to explain why it happens.

FOR YOU TO READ

The Language of Electricity

Now you are ready to become acquainted with some of the basic language of electricity. You are ready to learn the meanings of, and use, some of the "electricity words" that you identified in Activity 1. Here are some theories and definitions about electricity to help you:

• There are two kinds of electric charges, positive and negative, named by Benjamin Franklin. Protons have positive charge, and electrons have negative charge. Like kinds of electric charge repel, and unlike kinds attract.

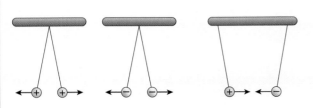

Like charges repel, and opposite charges attract.

• There is a smallest amount of the property called electric charge, the amount possessed by 1 proton and 1 electron. While protons and electrons differ in several ways (such as mass), an electron and a proton have an identical amount of charge.

• It is electrons that move in electric circuits of the kind you have been exploring. They flow through the circuit path, delivering energy, often in the form of heat and light, as they go. Protons, although present in the materials from which circuits are made, do not flow because they are locked within atoms. Positive particles sometimes do move in circuits where part of the path is liquid or gas.

• Scientists have agreed upon a standard "package" of electric charge, called the coulomb. Just as 12 eggs are called a dozen, 6.25 billion-billion basic charges are called a coulomb. To provide a sense of how big this number is, one coulomb is approximately the charge transferred during a lightning bolt!

• Scientists have agreed upon a standard rate of flow of the electric "current" in circuits. When one coulomb of charge passes through a point in a circuit during each second of time, the current is said to be one ampere, symbol A, or often abbreviated to amp.

- Different materials offer different resistance, or opposition, to the flow of electric current through them. Tungsten, from which light bulb filaments are made, has high electrical resistance. When current flows through it, the tungsten metal "robs" energy from the moving electrons and gets hot. Copper, by contrast, has low resistance; electrons transfer very little energy when flowing through copper. Electrical resistance is measured in ohms(Ω).

- Batteries or the hand generator provide energy to the electrons. These electrons are then able to light bulbs, heat wires, or make motors turn. The energy given to each coulomb of charge is measured in volts (V).

REFLECTING ON THE ACTIVITY AND THE CHALLENGE

In this activity you were introduced to the parallel and series circuits and to the electrical terms which you will need to know and be able to use for planning electric circuits to be used in the universal dwelling.

It is a fact that homes are "wired" using parallel circuits. Individual houses, apartments, mobile homes, or any other dwellings that receive electricity from a power company, have circuits of the parallel kind. Some older homes have as few as four circuits, and newer homes usually have many more. Each circuit in a home may have several light bulbs and other electrical appliances "plugged in," all in parallel. When electrical appliances are hooked up in parallel, if one is off or diconnected, the others can still be on. In a series circuit, if any appliance is disconnected, the other appliances cannot work. In your training manual, you will need to explain why the circuits in the universal dwelling are wired in parallel.

PHYSICS TO GO

1. What kind of circuit, series or parallel, would you choose for household wiring, and why? Write a short paragraph to explain your choice.

2. Did the generator used in this activity seem to have an "output limit?" In other words, did you arrive at conditions when the generator could not make the bulbs glow brightly even though you tried to crank the generator? Discuss this in a few sentences.

3. There is a great big generator at the power plant that sends electricity to your home. The wind generator chosen for HFE is much smaller than the generators used at power plants, but much larger than the one used for this activity. What implications might the output limit of the HFE electrical system have for the number of light bulbs and other electrical appliances that can be used in the HFE appliance package that you will recommend? Discuss this in a short paragraph.

STRETCHING EXERCISES

Thomas Edison is arguably one of the greatest inventors in world history. When we think of Edison, we think of the light bulb and the changes that this invention has made on the world. Edison dreamed of a world where we could read at night, where we could stroll down a lit street and where we could have daytime all the time. Electricity and the light bulb have made that dream a reality. We live in Edison's dream!

Edison once said that genius is 1% inspiration and 99% perspiration. Explain the meaning of this phrase.

Construct a list of Edison's major inventions. (Edison had 1,903 patents in his name!)

Activity Three
Load Limit

WHAT DO YOU THINK?

Everybody has at one time "blown a fuse" or "tripped" a circuit breaker.

- **What is a fuse or circuit breaker?**
- **Exactly what conditions do you think make a fuse "blow" or a circuit breaker "trip?"**

Record your ideas about these questions in your *Active Physics log*. Be prepared to discuss your responses with your small group and the class.

FOR YOU TO DO

1. Your teacher will do this part of the activity as a demonstration for the entire class. You will intentionally exceed the load limit of the circuits that supply electricity to your classroom. Observe the number of light bulbs needed to reach the load limit and the manufacturer's ratings of the bulbs.

   a) Calculate the load limit of the circuit, in watts. This will apply to the load limit of the circuits for your Homes For Everyone (HFE) dwelling.

2. Knowing that the energy per unit of electric charge supplied to the circuit is 120 V (volts), use the answer to the previous calculation and the equation

   Power = current × voltage ($P = IV$)

   to calculate the current, in amperes, that must have been flowing in the circuit when the load limit was reached.

   a) Show your calculation in your log. Assume a voltage of 120 V.

   b) How much current, in amps, must be flowing through the filament of a 60-W light bulb when it is operating in a 120-V household circuit? A 100-W light bulb? Show your calculations in your log.

   c) Fuses and circuit breakers are rated in amperes, usually 15 or 20 A for most household circuits. In your log use the equation $P = IV$ to show how you can calculate the load limit, in watts, of a 120-V household circuit protected by a 15-A circuit breaker.

PHYSICS TALK

The power supplied to a circuit can be calculated using the following equation:

$$P = IV$$

where P is power in watts (W),

I is current in amperes (A), and

V is voltage in volts (V)

This equation may be rearranged to calculate the value of any of the terms.

$$I = \frac{P}{V} \qquad V = \frac{P}{I}$$

Example:

A current of 0.83 A flows in a light bulb operating in a 120-V circuit. Calculate the power of the light bulb.

$$
\begin{aligned}
P &= IV \\
&= 0.83\ \text{A} \times 120\ \text{V} \\
&= 100\ \text{W}
\end{aligned}
$$

REFLECTING ON THE ACTIVITY AND THE CHALLENGE

The load limit of the electrical system for the universal dwelling is set at 2400 W, as outlined in the chapter scenario. It is also established by the design of the windmill power plant that 120 V will be applied to circuits within the dwelling. In this activity you learned what load limit means, and how to relate it to current and voltage. If the people in the dwelling try to run appliances that require more than 2400 W, the fuse will blow. In your home, you can always choose a different line to run the extra appliances. With only one generator, this is not an option in the universal dwelling. This will have direct application soon when you begin selecting appliances to be used in the dwelling.

⚠ **Make sure small appliances are unplugged before handling them.**

PHYSICS TO GO

1. Explain in detail what load limit means, and include maximum current, in amperes, as part of your explanation.

2. Find out about the power rating, in watts, of at least six electrical appliances. You can do this at home, at a store that sells appliances, or by studying a catalog. Some appliances have the watt rating stamped somewhere on the device itself, but for others you may have to check the instruction book for the appliance or find the power rating on the original package. Also, your local power company probably will provide a free list of appliances and their power ratings on request. Bring your list to class.

   If the appliance lists the current in amps, you can assume a voltage of 120 V and calculate the power (in watts) by using the equation $P = VI$.

3. List three appliances you would include in the HFE appliance package that will be part of the chapter assessment. For each appliance, list the power demand. For each appliance, describe how it will contribute to the well being of the people living in the dwelling.

4. An electric hair dryer has a power rating of 1200 W and is designed to be used on a 120 V household circuit. How much current flows in the dryer when it is in use?

5. A 120-V circuit for the kitchen of a home is protected by a 20 A circuit breaker. What combinations of the below appliances can be used on the circuit at the same time without the circuit breaker shutting off the circuit?
   - 1000 W toaster
   - 1200 W frying pan
   - 300 W blender
   - 600 W coffee maker

6. How many 60-W incandescent light bulbs can be operated at the same time on a 120 V, 15 A circuit in a home? How many energy-efficient 22-W fluorescent bulbs can operate on a similar circuit?

7. Some electrical appliances are rated in horsepower (HP).

$$1 \text{ HP} = 746 \text{ W}$$

What amount of current flows in a 0.8 HP vacuum cleaner operating on a 120 V circuit?

8. Some electrical appliances are rated in amps. What is the power in watts of a 6 A appliance designed to operate on a 120 V circuit?

STRETCHING EXERCISE

Find out about the electrical system of your home or the home of a friend or acquaintance. **With the approval of the owner or manager, and with adult supervision,** locate the load center, also called the main distribution panel, for the electrical system. Open the panel door and observe whether the system uses circuit breakers or fuses. How many are there, and what is the ampere rating shown on each fuse or circuit breaker? You may find some larger fuses or breakers that control large, 240-V appliances such as a kitchen range (electric stove); if so, how many are there, what are their ampere ratings, and, if you can, determine what they control.

In some load centers there is a list of what rooms or electrical devices are controlled by each fuse or breaker, but often the list is missing or incomplete.

With the approval of the owner or manager, and with adult supervision, you can develop a list that indicates what each fuse or breaker controls. To do so, shut off one circuit and go through the entire house to find the lights and outlets that are "dead" (check outlets with a lamp that you can carry around easily). Those items that are "off" are controlled by that fuse or breaker. List them. Then repeat the same process.

Report your findings to your teacher in the form of a list or diagram of the house showing what is controlled by each fuse or circuit breaker.

Warning: The inside of a load center is a dangerous area. Do not touch anything. Doing so could cause injury or death. Always have a qualified person help you.

Do not touch any exposed electrical connections or wiring harnesses. Do not attempt to look into or insert anything into any wiring entry points on the panel. Do not reset any circuit breakers or attempt to change any fuses.

Activity Four
Who's In Control?

WHAT DO YOU THINK?

Many electrical switches are operated manually (by hand), and many others are automatic, turning appliances on and off in response to a variety of conditions.

- **List as many different kinds of automatic switching devices as you can.**

- **What are the conditions that cause the on/off action of the switch?**

Record your ideas about this question in your *Active Physics log*. Be prepared to discuss your responses with your small group and the class.

FOR YOU TO DO

1. Assemble the circuit as shown in the diagram. (Each number corresponds to a different wire.)

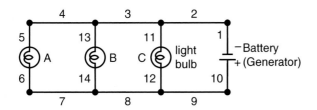

✎ a) Draw a diagram of the circuit. Label the bulbs: A, B, C. (The bulb on the left should be A, the bulb in the middle B, and the bulb on the right C.)

2. Compare the circuit you assembled with the one in the following diagram that shows the circuit that you used in Activity 2. This time you used additional wires, 14 wires in total. It is sometimes easier to place switches into circuits if you use a few additional wires in the circuit. Crank the generator to be sure that all bulbs operate in this circuit.

 **Have your teacher approve your circuit before proceeding.**

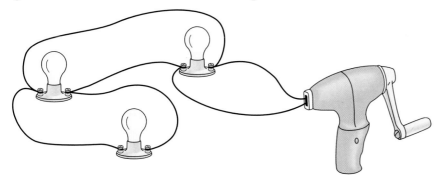

✎ a) Identify the additional new wires on your circuit diagram.
✎ b) What type of circuit (series or parallel) is represented in both diagrams?

3. Predict which wire could be replaced with a switch if you wished to turn all three bulbs on and off.

✎ a) Record your prediction in your log.
✎ b) Replace that wire with a switch. Does it work as predicted?

4. Predict which wire could be replaced with a switch if you wished to turn only bulb A on and off?

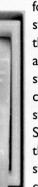 a) Record your prediction in your log.

b) Replace that wire with a switch. Does it work as predicted?

c) Mark the location of the switch on the circuit diagram in your log by writing "Switch A" and drawing an arrow from the word "Switch A" to the place where the switch should be placed.

5. Repeat Step 4 for bulb B and then for bulb C.

a) Remember to record your predictions.

b) Replace the wire you chose with a switch. Are your predictions beginning to improve?

c) Draw two addition diagrams to show the location of switch B and switch C.

FOR YOU TO READ

Switches

Regardless of how an electrical switch may be activated, most switches work in the same basic way. When a switch is "on," a good conductor of electricity, usually copper, is provided as the path for current flow through the switch. Then, the circuit containing the switch is said to be "closed," and the current flows. When a switch is turned "off," the conducting path through the switch is replaced by an air gap. Since air has very high resistance, the current flow through the switch is interrupted, and the circuit is said to be "open."

Circuit Diagrams

An electrical circuit can be represented by a simple line diagram, called a schematic diagram, or wiring diagram. You may have seen wiring diagrams for cars, stereo systems, or homes. They may appear complicated, but if you know what the different symbols represent, they are relatively easy to follow.

The wire that carries the electric current is represented by a straight line. If a wire crosses over another wire, a line crossing a straight line is shown. If the wires join, a heavy black dot is shown. A lamp or light bulb is shown by a loop in the center of a circle. A battery or a generator is represented by a number of unequal lines. A switch is a line shown at an angle to the wire. There are many other symbols that are used by electricians.

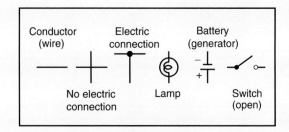

REFLECTING ON THE ACTIVITY AND THE CHALLENGE

Part of the problem you are facing with the electrical system for the HFE dwellings is to assure that the people who live in them will not exceed the 2400 W power limit of the system by having too many appliances in use at any one time. Depending on what you choose to include in the HFE appliance package, it may be necessary to use switching devices—automatic, manual, or both—to assure that the people who live in the homes will stay within the power limit as they use their appliances.

Perhaps you could also use automatic switches as "fail safe" devices to prevent accidentally using up too much electrical energy by, for example, forgetting to shut off lights that are not in use.

PHYSICS TO GO

1. In your log, describe several possibilities for using switching devices to address the power limit problem in your universal dwelling. Write your ideas in your log.

2. Electric switches are available which act as timers to turn appliances on and off at chosen times or for chosen intervals. Identify one or more ways a timer switch would be useful in an HFE dwelling.

3. Look at the wiring diagrams shown. Copy each into your log. Position and draw a switch in each circuit which would allow you to turn one light on, and leave two lights off.

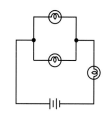

STRETCHING EXERCISES

Shop, in a store or catalog, for electrical switching devices controlled by a variety of conditions such as light/dark, high/low temperature, motion, etc. The devices may be either "built-in" to appliances (example: waterbed thermostat) or separate (example: a clock timer designed to control appliances plugged into it). Find as many different kinds of switching devices as you can, and note which ones may be useful for the HFE electrical system, and for what purpose. In your log, write a brief report on your findings.

Activity Five
Cold Shower

WHAT DO YOU THINK?

The entire daily energy output of an HFE generator would not be enough to heat water for an average American family for a day.

- **If an electrical heating coil (a type of resistor) were submerged in a container of water, and if a current were to flow through the coil to make it hot, what factors would affect the temperature increase of the water? Identify as many factors as you can, and predict the effect of each on the water temperature.**

Record your ideas about this question in your *Active Physics log*. Be prepared to discuss your responses with your small group and the class.

FOR YOU TO DO

1. Assemble and use an electric calorimeter according to the directions given by your teacher. Add a measured amount of cold tap water to the calorimeter.

   a) Record the mass of the water. (You will need to find the mass of an empty container as well as the mass of the container and the measured amount of water.)

   b) Measure and record the temperature of the water.

   c) Record the watt rating of the resistor that will be used to heat the water.

2. Mark the time at which you begin sending electric current through the resistor. Keep the electric heater operating for the amount of time recommended by your teacher. When you stop the current, note the time, stir the water, and measure the final, maximum temperature of the water.

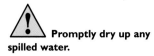 **Always make sure the coil (or heater) is completely submerged in the water.**

Promptly dry up any spilled water.

Do not try to stir the water with the thermometer. If the thermometer should break, immediately notify your instructor.

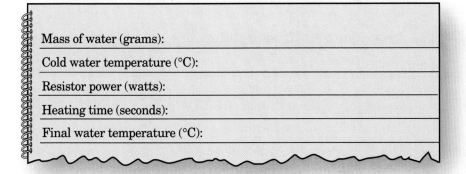

Mass of water (grams):

Cold water temperature (°C):

Resistor power (watts):

Heating time (seconds):

Final water temperature (°C):

a) In your log record the final water temperature (°C) and the heating time (seconds).

3. The heat energy gained by an object can be found using the equation:

Heat energy = mass of object × specific heat of material × temperature change

Use the equation to calculate the heat energy gained by the water in the calorimeter. The specific heat of water is 4180 J/kg.°C.

a) Show your calculation in your log.

4. Power rating, in watts, is expressed as the amount of energy that something consumes per unit of time. Mathematically, power is expressed as

$$\text{Power} = \frac{\text{energy}}{\text{time}}$$

Then it is true that: Energy = power × time

Energy can be expressed in kilowatt-hours (kWh) if power is in kilowatts and time is in hours, OR energy can be expressed in joules, if power is expressed in watts, and time in seconds. Use the equation to calculate the electrical energy, in joules, consumed by the resistor in the calorimeter.

a) Show your calculation in your log.

5. The energy calculated from the temperature change of the water should be equal to the energy calculated from the power rating of the appliance and the time.

a) Compare these two values for the heat energy. If the values are not the same, what must you conclude?

b) Where could the "lost" energy have gone?

6. If all of the electrical energy did not heat up the water, then you know your system for heating water is less than 100% efficient. Calculate the efficiency of your water heating device. (Hint: If the appliance were 100% efficient, all of the electrical energy would have heated the water; if the appliance were 50% efficient, half of the electrical energy would have heated the water.)

a) Record your calculations in you log. How efficient was the calorimeter?

PHYSICS TALK

Energy, E, in joules, can be calculated using the following equation.

$$E = VIt$$

where V is voltage in volts,

I is current in amperes, and

t is time.

If time is given in seconds, energy units are watt-seconds or joules. If time is given in hours, energy units are watts-hours and can be converted to kilowatt-hours

Since $P = IV$, the equation above may be written as:

$$E = Pt$$

Example:

A 100 W electric heat coil is used to heat a cup of cold water for 8 min (8 min = (8×60)s) to make a hot chocolate drink. Calculate the energy used by the heat coil.

$E = Pt$

$= 100 \text{ W} \times 480 \text{ s}$

$= 48,000 \text{ J (joules)}$

Heat energy is measured in units of joules (J). The heat energy gained by an object can be found using the following equation.

Heat energy = mass of object $\times$ specific heat of material $\times$ temperature change

where heat energy is expressed in joules (J),

mass is in kilograms (kg),

specific heat in joules per kilogram degree Celsius (J/kg.°C),

temperature in degrees Celsius (°C).

→

You may also see this equation written as follows.

$$E_H = mc\Delta T$$

The symbol for specific heat is c. The symbol Δ represents a change in something, in this case, temperature.

To calculate the heat energy gained by a material, you must know the specific heat of the material. Different materials require different amounts of energy to raise the temperature of a given mass of the substance. Different substances have different capacities to hold heat. Water holds heat very well, whereas silver does not hold heat well. Water is said to have a higher specific heat than silver. The specific heat of a material is the amount of energy required to raise 1 kg of the material by 1°C.

The specific heat of water is 4180 J/kg.°C

REFLECTING ON THE ACTIVITY AND THE CHALLENGE

In this activity your knowledge of how to calculate electric power consumption was extended to include how to calculate electric energy consumption. You also learned that heating water electrically requires a lot of energy and can be quite inefficient. All of this knowledge applies directly to the selections you will make for electrical appliances to be used in the universal dwelling.

PHYSICS TO GO

1. The calorimeter did not allow the water to trap 100% of the energy delivered to it by the resistor. Some of the heat energy probably escaped from the water. Identify and explain ways in which you think heat energy may have escaped from the water, reducing the efficiency of the calorimeter.

2. The calorimeter used in this activity can be thought of as a scaled-down, crude version of a household hot water heater. The efficiencies of hot water heaters used in homes range from about 80% for older models to as much as 92% for new, energy-efficient models. Identify and explain ways in which you think heat escapes from household hot water heaters, and how some of the heat loss could be prevented.

3. From what you have learned so far, discuss the possibilities for providing electrically heated water for Homes For Everyone (HFE). Is a standard water heater of the kind used in American homes desirable, or possible, for HFE? What other electrical options exist for accomplishing part or all of the task of heating water for HFE?

4. For most Americans, the second biggest energy user in the home, next to the heating/air conditioning system, is the water heater. A family of four that heats water electrically (some use gas or oil to heat water) typically spends about $35 per month using a 4500-W heater to keep a 160 L (40 gallon) tank of water hot at all times. The water is raised from an average inlet temperature of 10°C (50°F) to a temperature of 60°C (140°F), and the average family uses about 250 L (60 gallons) of hot water per day for bathing and washing clothes and dishes.

   In the above description, explain what each of the following numbers represents: 35, 4500, 160, 40, 10, 50, 60, 140, 250, 60.

5. Make a list with three columns in your log. The first column will be Name of Appliance, the second column will be Power (Watts), the third column will be Form of Energy Delivered.

Choose 5 appliances from the list of Home Electrical Appliances beginning on page H72 that have a wide range of power. Use information from the list of appliances to fill in the first two columns. In the third column, write the form of energy (heat, light, motion, sound, etc.) that you think each appliance is designed to deliver.

What pattern, if any, do you think exists between the power rating of an appliance and the form of energy it is designed to provide? Explain your answer.

6. Make a new list with 6 columns similar to the one shown.

Choose 5-10 appliances from the list. Record the name and power rating of that appliance. Record the approximate time that this appliance is used in one day. Calculate the time that this appliance is used in one month (assuming that a month has 30 days). Calculate the electrical energy that the appliance consumes.

The energy in watt-hours (Wh) is found by multiplying the power times the time in hours in one month.

$$\text{Energy} = \text{power} \times \text{time}$$

Calculate the energy in kilowatt-hours (kWh) by dividing the watt-hours by 1000 since there are 1000 W in a 1 kW.

Appliance	Power (Watts)	#hours/ day (est.)	#hours/ month	Energy/month (Wh/month)	Energy/month (kWh/month)

STRETCHING EXERCISE

1. Find out about EnergyGuide labels. Recently, the US government established a federal law that requires EnergyGuide labels to be displayed on major appliances such as water heaters, refrigerators, freezers, dishwashers, clothes washers, air conditioners, furnaces, and heat pumps. The bright yellow EnergyGuide label allows consumers to compare the energy costs and efficiencies of appliances. Visit a store where appliances are sold and record the information given on the EnergyGuide labels of competing brands of one kind of appliance, such as water heaters. Prepare a short report on which appliance you would purchase, and why.

2. Research ways to reduce the amount of electrical energy needed to provide hot water for your own home or an HFE dwelling. Some possibilities may include (a) using solar energy and/or a "tempering tank" to heat the water partially, followed by "finishing off" the heating electrically, and (b) tankless "instant" water heaters which use electricity to heat water, but only when hot water is needed. Prepare a report on your findings.

Home Electrical Appliances

Average Power and
Average Monthly Energy Use for a Family of Four

Family Data

	Power (watts)	Energy/mo. (kWh/mo.)
Big Appliances		
Air Conditioner		
(Room)	1,360	
(Central)	3,540	
Clothes Washer	512	
Clothes Dryer	5,000	
Dehumidifier	645	
Dishwasher	1,200	
Freezer	400	
Humidifier	177	
Pool Filter	1,000	
Kitchen Range	12,400	
Refrigerator	795	
Space Heater	1,500	
Waterbed	350	
Water Heater	4,500	
Small Refrigerator	300	
Lights & Minor Appliances (combined)		
Kitchen		
Baby Food Warmer	165	
Blender	300	
Broiler (portable)	1,200	
Can Opener	100	
Coffee Maker		
Drip	1,100	
Percolator	600	
Corn Popper		
Oil-type	575	
Hot Air-type	1,400	
Deep Fryer	1,500	
Food Processor	370	
Frying Pan	1,200	
Garbage Disposal	445	
Sandwich Grill	1,200	
Hot Plate	1,200	
Microwave Oven	750	
Mixer	150	

Home Electrical Appliances

	Power (watts)	Energy/mo. (kWh/mo.)
Roaster	1,400	
Rotisserie	1,400	
Slow Cooker	200	
Toaster	1,100	
Toaster-Oven	1,500	
Trash Compactor	400	
Waffle Iron	1,200	
Entertainment		
Computer	60	
Radio	70	
Television	90	
Stereo	125	
VCR	50	
Personal Care		
Air Cleaner	50	
Curling Iron	40	
Hair Dryer	1,200	
Hair Rollers	350	
Heat Blanket	170	
Heat Lamp	250	
Heat Pad	60	
Iron	1,100	
Lighted Mirror	20	
Shaver	15	
Sun Lamp	300	
Toothbrush	1	
Miscellaneous		
Auto Engine Heater	850	
Clock	3	
Drill (1/4")	250	
Fan (attic)	375	
Fan (window)	200	
Heat Tape	240	
Sewing Machine	75	
Skill Saw	1,000	
Vacuum Cleaner	650	
Water Pump (well)	335	

Please note: Average values of power are shown. The power of a particular appliance may vary considerably from the value in the table. Energy use will vary with family size (a four-member family is assumed for the tabled values), personal preferences and habits, climate, and season. Similar information in greater detail is available free upon request from most electric utilities.

HOME

Activity Six
Pay Up

WHAT DO YOU THINK?

Eggs are priced by the dozen, and electricity is priced by the kilowatt-hour.

- **What factors determine the amount of money the electric company charges you for the use of an appliance?**

Record your ideas about this question in your *Active Physics log*. Be prepared to discuss your responses with your small group and the class.

FOR YOU TO DO

1. Look at the copies of the electrical bills provided. If possible, also obtain a copy of the monthly electric bill for your home or that of an acquaintance. Compare the electric bills provided below, or the ones from the homes of individuals in your group.

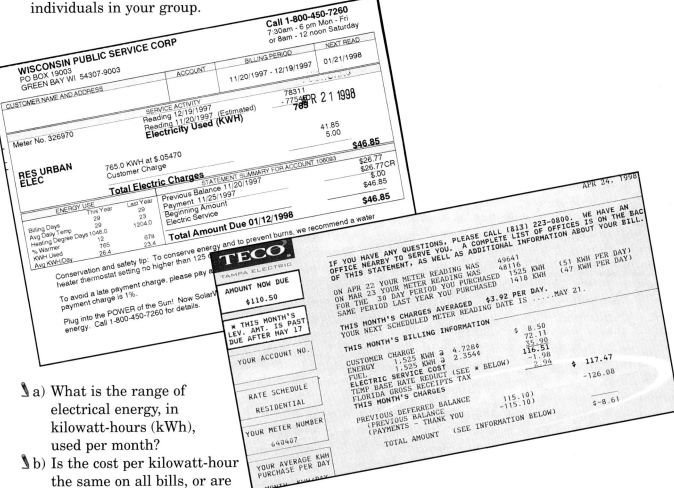

🖊 a) What is the range of electrical energy, in kilowatt-hours (kWh), used per month?

🖊 b) Is the cost per kilowatt-hour the same on all bills, or are there differences?

🖊 c) What factors might account for differences among electric bills within your group? Identify as many factors as you can and explain what you think is the effect of each factor on the bill.

🖊 d) What is the average monthly amount of electrical energy used in the homes represented in your group, and how does it compare to the 90 kWh per month available to HFE dwellings?

CHAPTER 2

2. In Activity 5, you estimated the time that an appliance is used, and the amount of energy required to use it for one month. Now you will calculate the expense of that energy. Combine the lists from the group members and calculate the expense of running the electrical appliances by using the following equation:

Cost = Energy × Price per unit of energy

The price for electricity can be taken from the electric bills that were provided.

a) Record your calculations in your log.

3. Compare the cost of electricity in your town to other places in the United States. The "low" for electrical costs is approximately $0.03 (3 cents) per kWh. The "high" for electrical costs is approximately $0.16 (16 cents) per kWh.

a) What are the high and low costs of the electrical bills which you examined?

b) How might your consumption of electricity change if you had to pay for your own electrical bills?

FOR YOU TO READ

Determining Energy Consumption

The electrical energy consumed by appliances can be determined in different ways. If the power rating of an appliance is known, and if the power remains at a steady value while the appliance is in use (example: light bulb), the energy, in kWh, can be calculated by multiplying the power of the appliance, in kilowatts, by the time, in hours, for which the appliance is used (Energy = Power × Time).

Determining the energy consumed by some appliances, however, is tricky, because the appliances vary in power while they are in use. For example, a refrigerator may cycle on and off under the control of a thermostat. Therefore, it is not operating during all of the time it is "plugged

in," and the calculation described above would lead to a misleadingly high value for the heater's energy consumption. For such appliances whose power varies throughout time, a kilowatt-hour meter is used to measure the total energy consumed, with variations in power throughout time taken into account. The same kind of meter, a kilowatt-hour meter, is used by the power company to measure the total electrical energy used in your home. The meter is mounted somewhere at your home so that it can be read by the power company's "meter reader" person.

Another way to determine the energy used by electrical appliances is to use the experience of power companies or corporations that sell electrical supplies. Extensive lists of appliances, their power ratings, and each appliance's average energy use per month by a typical family are available free from such sources.

PHYSICS TALK

The cost of operating an electrical appliance can be calculated using the following equation.

Cost = Energy × Price per unit of energy

where energy is in kilowatt-hours
(1000 watt-hours = 1 kWh).

Example:

An electric coffee maker uses an average of 22.5 kWh of energy each month. If the family is charged 12¢/kWh for electricity, what is the average monthly cost of operating the coffee maker?

Cost = Energy × Price per unit of energy

= 22.5 kWh x $0.12/kWh

= $2.70

REFLECTING ON THE ACTIVITY AND THE CHALLENGE

In this activity you learned that the average American family's energy use exceeds the maximum available for our HFE dwellings. Imagine how your own standard of living would change if you were restricted to 90 kWh per month.

The challenge requires that you need to be thinking about two things at the same time as you select appliances for the universal dwelling: the power consumed by each appliance and the amount of time for which each appliance is used. Both need to be taken into account to stay within the power and energy limits of the HFE electrical system.

PHYSICS TO GO

1. A 1200-W hair dryer is used by several members of a family for a total of 30 min per day during a 30-day month. How much electrical energy is consumed by the dryer during the month? Give your answer in

   a) watt-hours
   b) kilowatt-hours.

2. If the power company changes $0.15 per kWh for electrical energy, what is the cost of using the hair dryer in question 1 during the month? What is the cost for a year?

3. Not enough heat from the furnace reaches one bedroom in a home. The homeowner uses a portable 1350 W electric heater 24 hours per day to keep the bedroom warm during four cold winter months. At $0.12 per kilowatt-hour, how much does it cost to operate the heater for the four months? (Assume two 30-day and two 31-day months.)

4. Prepare your personal list of electrical appliances to recommend to your group to be included in the HFE appliance package. Remember that you will have to justify why you chose a certain appliance. Be prepared to contribute your ideas to your group's decision-making process when completing the challenge.

5. A portable CD player is approximately 20 W and uses 4 AA batteries.

   a) Estimate the number of hours that you can listen to the music on a CD player before the batteries need replacing.
   b) Calculate the energy requirements of the CD player.
   c) Estimate the cost of 4 AA batteries.
   d) Calculate the cost per kilowatt hour of a battery.
   e) Compare battery costs with the cost of electricity from the utilities (use approximately 10¢ per kilowatt hour).

Activity Seven
More for Your Money

WHAT DO YOU THINK?

Some hot water heaters and furnaces for homes are more than 90% efficient.

- **If high-efficiency appliances cost more, are they worth the added cost?**

Record your ideas about this question in your *Active Physics log*. Be prepared to discuss your responses with your small group and the class.

FOR YOU TO DO

1. Place one liter of cold tap water in a beaker made of Pyrex glass. Make sure the outside of the beaker is dry so it does not slip from your grasp. Measure the temperature of the water.

 a) Record the temperature of the water in your log.

  b) Record the quantity of water in milliliters and grams. (1 mL of water has a mass of 1 g.)

2. Place the beaker of water in a microwave oven of known power, in watts. Mark the time at which the oven is turned on at its highest power level. After two minutes, stop the time measurement. Carefully check that the beaker is not too hot to grasp and remove the beaker from the oven, stir the water, and check the water temperature, all as quickly as possible.

microwave oven power = _____ watts

time required to heat water = _____ seconds

final water temperature = _____ °C

a) Record the following in your log:

b) Why is it important to complete the temperature measurement as quickly as possible?

3. Prepare an identical Pyrex beaker containing the same amount of cold tap water, preferably at the same original temperature as the water used above.

a) Record the mass and temperature of the water in your log.

4. Have ready a hot plate that has not been turned on (a "cold" hot plate) and that has a known power rating, in watts. Also have ready a clock or stopwatch capable of measuring time, in seconds, for an interval of several minutes. Place the beaker of cold water on the hot plate, and mark the time at which the hot plate is turned on at its highest setting. Gently stir the water while it is heating and monitor the temperature of the water. When the temperature of the water has increased to the value of the water from the microwave, mark the time and shut the hot plate off.

a) Record the power of the hot plate, the time required to heat the water, and its final temperature in your log.

5. Repeat the process a third time with the coil.

a) Record all your observations in your log.

6. Energy (in joules) = Power (in watts) × Time (in seconds)

Calculate the energy used by each appliance to cause
equal temperature increases in equal amounts of water.

a) Show your calculations in your log.

b) Which appliance is the "winner"? Choose a way to express
a comparison of the performance of the three appliances.

c) Was the method used to compare the three appliances
fair? How could the fairness be improved?

d) The beaker that served as the container for the water also
was heated by the three appliances. Did it affect the
outcome of the comparison? Might another kind of
container be more or less effective to use with either
appliance; for example, might using a metal pan as the
container on a hot plate make the hot plate perform more
efficiently?

REFLECTING ON THE ACTIVITY
AND THE CHALLENGE

You know that the electrical appliances used in the universal
dwelling cannot exceed 90 kWh per month of energy
consumption. In this activity you discovered that some
appliances are more efficient than others. That is, a highly
efficient appliance can accomplish a task while using less
electrical energy than a low-efficiency appliance for the same
task. Obviously you will want to make a careful selection for
each kind of appliance based on efficiency so that HFE
inhabitants can have the greatest possible benefit from the
electrical system.

PHYSICS TO GO

1. Are some cooking utensils (pots, pans, etc.) better than others for certain purposes? Write what you think about the effectiveness of different cooking utensils, and what you could do to find out about their comparative effects on efficiency.

2. Does either the hot plate or the microwave oven seem to be a good choice to include in the HFE appliance package? Why, or why not?

3. You probably have concluded that the most efficient appliance of the three tested is the one that used the least energy, but do you know the actual efficiency of the appliances? Explain how you could calculate the efficiencies, and try it. (Hint: See Activity 5.)

4. Calculate the energy used, in joules, by each of the following:
   a) a 1500 W hair dryer operating for 3 min,
   b) a 1200 W hair dryer operating for 4 min.

5. If both situations described in question 4 result in the same dryness of hair, which hair dryer is more efficient?

6. A 10 A electric pencil sharpener is used 2 min every working day.
   a) Calculate the power of the electric pencil sharpener.
   b) How much energy is used by the sharpener in one day?
   c) How much energy could be saved in one year (assume 5 working days per week all year) by using a manual pencil sharpener?

PHYSICS AT WORK

The Schultzes

LIVING CLEAN AND FREE

Bob-o Schultze and his family live "off-the-grid," miles from the nearest electrical power line. Their 2,400 square foot home in northern California includes two computers, a dishwasher, a microwave oven, a washing machine, and a satellite television. It is entirely powered by clean, free, renewable energy.

"Living off-the-grid does not require any major lifestyle changes," explains Mr. Schultze who has been living without traditional energy for over 30 years. "It takes no more technical sophistication or work than the basic up-keep of any house or car."

The Schultzes use three natural power sources: water, wind, and sun. There is a hydroelectric facility in a creek on the property, a wind machine behind the house, and photovoltaic facilities on tracks following the sun. All three feed into one large industrial, deep-cycle, 6-V battery and there is never an electric bill. "We are fortunate to have a great site, but every site has at least one source of natural, renewable, energy and most have two. The sun is always an option and if conditions allow for a wind machine, which must be 20-30 feet higher than anything within 500 feet, the power of the wind can also be harnessed."

"I was inspired by the Grateful Dead" explains Bob-o whose name was created from Robert by children many years ago and has stuck. "I moved to a very rural area—30 miles from any electrical power—and I wanted my music. I started using regular D batteries, which drained very quickly, then a car battery, which drained almost as quickly, and then I developed a hydroelectric plant."

All of the appliances in the Schultze's home are the most energy efficient available. "Compact florescent light uses only 25% of the power of standard lighting—and simply turning things off when they are not being used can save 500 Watt hours a day," says Bob-o, emphasizing that energy should be conserved regardless of its source. "We use nine to ten kilowatt hours per day, and the average for a family of four is about thirty. As more people become aware of the finite nature of traditional energy sources, the use of renewable energy will increase," claims Bob-o. The Schultzes are just a little ahead of many people in this regard.

Chapter 2 Assessment

You learned a great deal about electricity and electrical terms in this chapter. Read the scenario from the beginning of the chapter once again. Do you now understand all the terms used in the description of the wind-generator system?

Now that you have completed the activities in this chapter, you are ready to complete the chapter challenge. You will be asked to do the following.

- **List the appliances to be included in the HFE "appliance package." Your list must be as comprehensive as possible, and it must be clear how each appliance will enhance the health or well-being of the people who live in the dwelling.**

- **Develop an outline of the training manual for HFE volunteers. You manual must explain the difference between 2400 W and 3 kWh. It must also give clear examples of how use of the appliances in the package can be scheduled to stay within the power and energy limits of the electrical system on both a daily and a long-term basis.**

Review the criteria which you and your class established for how your appliance package and training manual will be graded. Your work will be judged on the basis of 100 points. If necessary, discuss the criteria once again, add details to the criteria if it would be helpful, and agree on the finalized point allocation.

Physics You Learned

Simple circuits

Generators

Series circuits

Parallel circuits

Power

$P=VI$ (watts)

Energy $= Pt$ (kilowatt-hours; joules)

Load limits

Fuses

Switches

Utility bills

Costs for electricity

Electrical efficiency

TOYS FOR
UNDERSTANDING

CHAPTER
3

Scenario

In this *Active Physics* chapter, you will try to help educate children through the use of toys. With your input, the Homes for Everyone (HFE) organization has developed an appliance package that will allow families living in the "universal dwelling" to enjoy a healthy and comfortable lifestyle. The HFE organization would now like to teach the children living in these homes, and elsewhere, more about electricity and the generation of electricity. They hope that this may encourage interest in children to use electricity wisely, as well as encourage development of alternative sources for electrical energy by future generations.

The HFE organization will work with a toy company to provide kits and instructions for children to make toy electric motors and generators. These toys should illustrate how electric motors and generators work and capture the interest of the children.

In an effort to help others, people often make changes or introduce new products without considering the personal and cultural impact on those whom they are trying to assist. If you ever become involved in a self-help community group, such as HFE, it would be important for you to work together with the people you are assisting to assess their needs, both personal and cultural. Although that is not possible given your limited time in class, you should recognize the need for collaborative teamwork in evaluating the impact of any new product on an established community.

Challenge

Your task is to prepare a kit of materials and instructions that the toy company will manufacture. Children will use these kits to make a motor or generator, or a combination electric motor/generator. It will serve both as a toy and to illustrate how the electric motors in home appliances work or how electricity can be produced from an energy source such as wind, moving water, a falling weight, or some other external source.

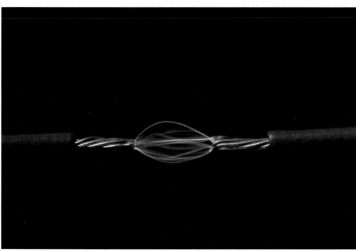

Criteria

Your work will be judged by the following criteria:

• **(30%) The motor/generator is made from inexpensive, common materials, and the working parts are exposed but with due consideration for safety.**

• **(40%) The instructions for the children clearly explain how to assemble and operate the motor/generator device, and explain how and why it works in terms of basic principles of physics.**

   • **(30%) If used as a motor, the device will operate using a maximum of four 1.5 V (volt) batteries (D cells), and will power a toy (such as a car, boat, crane, etc.) that will be fascinating to children.**

   OR

   • **(30%) If used as a generator, the device will demonstrate the production of electricity from an energy source such as wind, moving water, a falling weight, or some other external source and be fascinating to children.**

Activity One
The Electricity and Magnetism Connection

WHAT DO YOU THINK?

Generators produce electricity. Motors use electricity.

- **What is the significance of motors and generators to your standard of living? That is, how would your life be different if you had no motors or generators?**

Write your answer to this question in your *Active Physics log*. Be prepared to discuss your ideas with your small group and other members of your class.

FOR YOU TO DO

1. Set up the equipment as shown in the diagram, or as directed by your teacher.

2. The needle of a compass is a balanced magnet. It can be used as a magnetic field detector. If any magnet is present, the compass will respond. It usually aligns itself with Earth's magnetic field. With no current flowing in the wire, verify that the compass always points in the same direction, North, no matter where it is placed on the horizontal surface.

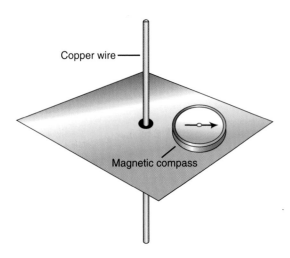

Copper wire

Magnetic compass

   a) Sketch the compass direction at different places on the horizontal surface in your log.

3. Bring another type of magnet, such as a bar magnet, into the area near the compass needle.

✎ a) Describe your observations in your log.

✎ b) What happens to the dependable north-pointing property of a compass when the compass is placed in a region where magnetic effects, in addition to Earth's magnetic field, exist?

4. You will now make a map of the magnetic field of the bar magnet. Place the magnet on another piece of paper and trace its position. Place the compass at one location and note the direction it points. Remove the compass.

✎ a) Put a small arrow at the location from which you removed the compass to signify the way in which the compass pointed.

✎ b) Place the compass at a second location about at the tip of the first arrow. Remove the compass and place another small arrow in this location to signify the way in which the compass pointed.

✎ c) Repeat the process at an additional 20 locations to get a map of the magnetic field of a bar magnet. Tape the piece of paper of the map in your log.

5. Return the compass to the horizontal surface surrounding the wire. Observe the orientation of the compass. Send a current through the wire. The direction of the flow of electrons which make up the current in the wire is from the negative terminal of the power supply to the positive terminal. Move the compass to different locations on the horizontal surface, observing the direction in which the compass points at each location. Make observations on all sides of the wire, and at different distances from the wire.

✎ a) Record how the compass was oriented when the bar magnet was removed.

✎ b) Describe any pattern that you observe about how the compass behaves when it is near the current-carrying wire. Use a sketch and words to describe your observations in your log.

✎ c) From your observations, what effect does the electric current appear to have on the wire?

⚠ **Do not adjust the power supply settings provided by your teacher.**

6. Reverse the direction of the current in the wire by exchanging the contacts of the power supply. Repeat your observations.

🖎 a) Describe the results.

🖎 b) Make up a rule for remembering the relationship between the direction of the current in a wire and the direction of the magnetism near the wire (i.e. when the current is up, the magnetic field . . .). Anyone told your rule should be able to use it with success. Write your rule in your log. Include a sketch. (Hint: One of the rules that physicists use makes use of your thumb and fingers.)

REFLECTING ON THE ACTIVITY AND THE CHALLENGE

This activity has provided you with knowledge about a critical link between electricity and magnetism, which is deeply involved in your challenge to make a working electric motor or generator. The response of the compass needle to a nearby electric current showed that an electric current itself has a magnetic effect which can cause a magnet, in this case a compass needle, to experience force. You have a way to go to understand and be able to be "in control" of electric motors and generators, but you've started along the path to being in control.

PHYSICS TO GO

1. If 100 compasses were available to be placed on the horizontal surface to surround the current-carrying wire in this activity, describe the pattern of directions in which the 100 compasses would point in each of the following situations:

   a) no current is flowing in the wire,
   b) a weak current is flowing in the wire,
   c) a strong current is flowing in the wire.

2. If a vertical wire carrying a strong current penetrated the floor of a room, and if you were using a compass to "navigate" in the room by always walking in the direction indicated by the north-seeking pole of the compass needle, describe the "walk" you would take.

3. Use the rule which you made up for remembering the relationship between the direction of the current flowing in a wire and the direction of the magnetic field near the wire to make a sketch showing the direction of the magnetic field near a wire which has a current flowing:

a) downward,
b) horizontally.

4. Physicists remember the orientation of the magnetic field of a current by placing their left thumb in the direction of the electron current and noting whether their fingers of the left hand curve clockwise or counterclockwise. Copy the following diagrams into your log. Use this rule to sketch the direction of the magnetic field in each case.

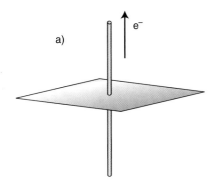

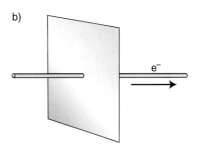

5. Imagine that a second vertical wire is placed in the apparatus used in this activity, but not touching the first wire. There is room to place a magnetic compass between the wires without touching either wire. If a compass were placed between the wires, in what direction would the compass point if the wires carry equal currents:

a) which are in opposite directions,
b) which are in the same direction.

6. A hollow, transparent plastic tube is placed on a horizontal surface as shown in the diagram. A wire carrying a current is wound once around the tube to form a circular loop in the wire. In what direction would a compass placed inside the tube point? (Plastic does not affect a compass; only the current in the wire loop will affect the compass.)

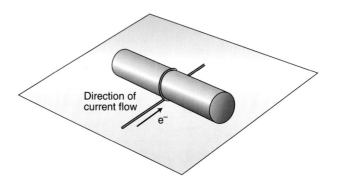

Direction of current flow

e⁻

STRETCHING EXERCISE

Use a compass to search for magnetic effects and magnetic "stuff." As you know, a compass needle usually aligns in a north-south direction (or nearly so, depending on where you live). If a compass needle does not align north-south, a magnetic effect in addition to that of the Earth is the cause, and the needle is responding to both the Earth's magnetism and some other source of magnetism. Use a compass as a probe for magnetic effects. Try to find magnetic effects in a variety of places and near a variety of things where you suspect magnetism may be present. Try inside a car, bus, or subway. The structural steel in some buildings is magnetized and may cause a compass to give a "wrong" reading. Try near the speaker of a radio, stereo, or TV. Try near electric motors, both operating and not operating.

Do not bring a known strong magnet close to a compass, because the magnet may change the magnetic alignment of the compass needle, destroying the effectiveness of the compass.

Make a list of the magnetic objects and effects that you find in your search.

Activity Two
Electromagnets

WHAT DO YOU THINK?

Large electromagnets are used to pick up cars in junk yards.

- **How does an electromagnet work?**
- **How could it be made stronger?**

Write your answer to this question in your *Active Physics log*. Be prepared to discuss your ideas with your small group and other members of your class.

FOR YOU TO DO

1. Wind 50 turns of wire on a drinking straw to form a solenoid as shown in the diagram on the next page. Use sandpaper to carefully clean the insulation from a short section of the wire ends to allow electrical connection of the solenoid to the generator.

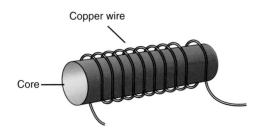

Copper wire

Core

2. Carefully connect the wires from the generator to the wire ends of the solenoid. Bring one end of the solenoid near the magnetic compass and crank the generator to send a current through the solenoid. Observe any effect on the compass needle. Try several orientations of the solenoid to produce effects on the compass needle.

  a) Record your observations in your log.
  b) How can you tell the "polarity" of an electromagnet; that is, how can you tell which end of an electromagnet behaves as a north-seeking pole?

3. Predict what you can do to change the polarity of an electromagnet.

  a) Write your answer in your log.
  b) Test your prediction.

4. Use the solenoid wound on the drinking straw as an electromagnet to pick up paper clips.

  a) Record your observations in your log.

5. Carefully, slip a nail into the drinking straw to serve as a new core. Again, test the effect on a compass needle.

  a) Record your observations in your log.

6. Use the solenoid wound on the nail to pick up paper clips.

  a) Record your observations in your log.
  b) What evidence did you find that the choice of core material for an electromagnet makes a difference?

7. Predict what will happen when you increase the current running through the coiled wire solenoid. This can be done by increasing the speed at which you crank the generator.

  a) Write your answer in your log.
  b) Test your prediction by measuring how many paper clips can be picked up.

8. Predict what will happen when you increase the number of turns of wire forming the solenoid.

  a) Write your answer in your log.
  b) Test your prediction by measuring how many paper clips can be picked up.

REFLECTING ON THE ACTIVITY AND THE CHALLENGE

An electromagnet, often constructed in the shape of a solenoid, and having an iron core, is the basic moving part of many electric motors. In this activity you learned how the amount of current and the number of turns of wire affect the strength of an electromagnet. You will be able to apply this knowledge to affect the speed and strength with which an electric motor of your own design rotates.

PHYSICS TO GO

1. Explain the differences between permanent magnets and electromagnets.

2. The diagram shows an electromagnet with a compass at each end. Copy the diagram and indicate the direction in which the compass needles will be pointing when a current is generated.

e −

3. Which of the following will pick up more paper clips when an electric current is sent through the wire:
   a) a coil of wire with 20 turns, or a coil of wire with 50 turns?
   b) wire wound around a cardboard core, or wire wound around a steel core?

4. Explain conditions necessary for two electromagnets to attract or repel one another, as do permanent magnets when they are brought near one another.

5. Explain what you think would happen if, when making an electromagnet, half of the turns of wire on the core were made in one direction, and half in the opposite direction.

STRETCHING EXERCISES

1. Find out how both permanent magnets and electromagnets are used. Do some library research to learn how electromagnets are used to lift steel in junk yards, make buzzers, or serve as part of electrical switching devices called "relays." For other possibilities, find out how magnetism is used in microphones and speakers within sound systems, or how "super-strong" permanent magnets made possible the small, high-quality, headset speakers for walkman radios and portable tape and CD players. Prepare a brief report on your findings.

2. Do some research to find out about "magnetic levitation." "Maglev" involves using super-conducting electromagnets to levitate, or suspend objects such as subway trains in air, thereby reducing friction and the "bumpiness" of the ride.

   a) What possibilities do "maglev" trains, cars, or other transportation devices have for the future?
   b) What advantages would such devices have?
   c) What problems need to be solved? Prepare a brief report on your research.

INQUIRY INVESTIGATION

Identify as many variables as you can which you think will affect the behavior of an electromagnet, and design an experiment to test the effect of each variable. Identify each variable, and describe what you would do to test its effects. After your teacher approves your procedures, do the experiments. Report your findings.

Activity Three
Detect and Induce Currents

WHAT DO YOU THINK?

In 1820, the Danish physicist Hans Christian Oersted placed a long, straight, horizontal wire on top of a magnetic compass. Both the compass and the wire were resting on a horizontal surface, and both the length of the wire and the compass needle were oriented north-south. Next, Oersted sent a current through the wire, and happened upon one of the greatest discoveries in physics.

• **What do you think Oersted saw?**

Write your answer to this question in your *Active Physics log*. Be prepared to discuss your ideas with your small group and other members of your class.

FOR YOU TO DO

1. Wrap 10 turns of wire to form a coil that surrounds a magnetic compass. Wrap the wire on a diameter corresponding to the north-south markings of the compass scale, as shown in the diagram. Hold the turns of wire in place with tape, or use the method recommended by your teacher. Use sandpaper to carefully remove the insulation from a short section of the wire ends to allow electrical connection.

2. In step 1, you constructed a galvanometer, a device to detect and measure small currents. Carefully connect a hand generator, a light bulb, and the galvanometer, as shown on page H98 (in a series circuit). Rest the galvanometer so that the compass is horizontal, with the needle balanced, pointing North, and free to rotate. Also, turn the galvanometer, if necessary, so that the compass needle is aligned parallel to the turns of wire which pass over the top of the compass.

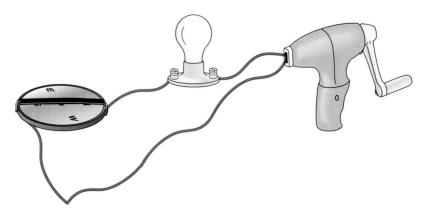

3. Crank the generator to establish a current in the circuit. Think of the compass needle as a meter such as the one in the speedometer of a car. The amount it moves corresponds to the amount of current. The glow of the light bulb verifies that current is flowing.

a) Does the compass-needle galvanometer also indicate that current is flowing? How? In your log, use words and a sketch to indicate your answer.

4. The amount of current flowing in the circuit can be varied by changing the speed at which the generator is cranked, and the amount of current is indicated by the brightness of the light bulb. Vary the speed at which you crank the generator, and observe the galvanometer.

a) How does the galvanometer indicate changes in the amount of current? Use words and sketches to indicate your answer.

5. Change the direction in which you crank the generator.

a) What evidence does the galvanometer provide that changing the direction in which the generator is cranked has the effect of changing the direction of current flow in the circuit? Use words and sketches to give your answer.

6. Carefully connect each wire end of a galvanometer to a wire end of a solenoid wound on a hollow core of nonmagnetic material, such as a cardboard tube. Orient the galvanometer so that it is ready to detect current flow.

7. Hold a bar magnet in one hand and the solenoid steady in the other hand. Rapidly plunge one end of the bar magnet into the hollow core of the solenoid, and then stop the motion of the magnet, bringing the end of the magnet to rest inside the solenoid. Another person should hold the galvanometer in a steady position so that it will not be disturbed if the solenoid is moved. Observe the galvanometer during the sequence. You may need to practice this a few times.

a) Write your observations in your log.

8. Remove the magnet from the solenoid with a quick motion, and observe the galvanometer during the action.

a) Record your observations.

b) A current is produced! How does the direction of the current caused, or induced, when the end of the magnet is entering the solenoid, compare to the direction of the current when the magnet is leaving the solenoid?

c) How can you detect the direction of the current in each case?

9. Modify and repeat steps 7 and 8 to answer the following questions.

a) What, if anything, about the created or induced current changes if the opposite end of the bar magnet is plunged in and out of the solenoid?

b) How does the induced current change if the speed at which the magnet is moved in and out of the solenoid is changed?

c) What is the amount of induced current when the magnet is not moving (stopped)?

d) What is the effect on the induced current of holding the magnet stationary and moving the solenoid back and forth over either end of the magnet?

e) What is the effect of moving both the magnet and the solenoid?

REFLECTING ON THE ACTIVITY AND THE CHALLENGE

In this activity you discovered that you can produce electricity. A current is created or induced when a magnet is moved in and out of a solenoid. The current flows back and forth, changing direction with each reversal of the motion of the magnet. Such a current is called an alternating current, and you may recognize that name as the kind of current that flows in household circuits. It is frequently referred to by its abbreviated form, "AC." It is the type of current that is used to run electric motors in home appliances. Part of your challenge is to explain to the children how a motor operates in terms of basic principles of physics or to show how electricity can be produced from an external energy source. This activity will help you with that part of the challenge.

PHYSICS TO GO

1. An electric motor takes electricity and converts it into movement. The movement can be a fan, a washing machine, or a CD player. The galvanometer may be thought of as a crude electric motor. Discuss that statement, using forms of energy as part of your discussion.

2. Explain how the galvanometer works to detect the amount and direction of an electric current.

3. How could the galvanometer be made more sensitive, so that it could detect very weak currents?

4. An electric generator takes motion and turns it into electricity. The electricity can then be used for many purposes. The solenoid and the bar magnet, as used in this activity could be thought of as a crude electric generator. Explain the truth of that statement, referring to specific forms of energy in your explanation.

5. If the activity were to be repeated so that you would be able to see only the galvanometer and not the solenoid, the magnet, and the person moving the equipment, would you be able to tell from only the response of the galvanometer what was being moved, the magnet or the solenoid or both? Explain your answer.

6. Part of the chapter challenge is to explain how the motor and generator toy works.

   a) Write a paragraph explaining how a motor works.
   b) Write a paragraph explaining how a generator works.

7. In generating electricity in this activity, you moved the magnet or the coil. How can you use each of the following resources to move the magnet?

   a) wind
   b) water
   c) steam

STRETCHING EXERCISE

Find out about the 120 V (volt) AC used in home circuits. If household current alternates, at what rate does it surge back-and-forth? Write down any information about AC that you can find and bring it to class.

Activity Four

AC & DC

WHAT DO YOU THINK?

In the last activity, you used human energy to produce motion to generate electricity.

• **What other kinds of energy can be used to generate electricity?**

Write your answer to this question in your *Active Physics log*. Be prepared to discuss your ideas with your small group and other members of your class.

FOR YOU TO DO

AC Generator

1. Your teacher will explain and demonstrate a hand-operated, alternating current (AC) generator. During the demonstration, make the observations necessary to gain the information needed to answer these questions:

🖎 a) When the AC generator is used to light a bulb, describe the brightness of the bulb when the generator is cranked slowly, and then rapidly. Write your observations in your log.

🖎 b) When the AC generator is connected to a galvanometer, describe the action of the galvanometer needle when the generator is cranked slowly, and then rapidly.

2. It is easier to understand the creation of a current if you think of a set of invisible threads to signify the magnetic field of the permanent magnets. The very thin threads fill the space and connect the north pole of one magnet with the south pole of the other magnet. If the wire of the generator is imagined to be a very thin, sharp knife, the question you must ask is whether the knife (the wire) can "cut" the threads (the magnetic field lines). If the wire moves in such a way that it can cut the field lines, then a current is generated. If the wire moves in such a way that it does not cut the field lines, then no current is generated.

a) Look at the diagrams of the magnetic fields shown. In which case, I, II, or III will a current be generated?

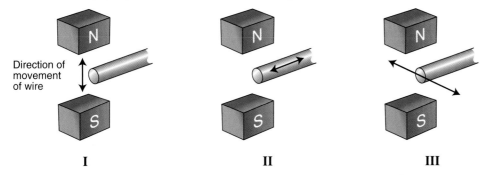

3. The following diagram shows the position of the rotating coil of an AC generator at instants separated by one-fourth of a rotation of the coil. Build a small model of the rectangular coil so that you can move the model to help you understand the drawings. The coil model can be constructed by carefully bending a coat hanger into the shape of the rectangular coil. Rest the coil between two pieces of paper—label the left paper N for the north pole of a magnet; label the right paper S for the south pole of a magnet.

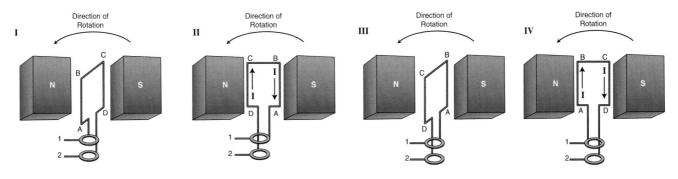

HOME

4. For the purpose of analyzing the rotating coil figure, the four sides of the rectangular coil of the AC generator will be referred to as sides AB, BC, CD, and DA. Side DA is "broken" to allow extension of the coil to the rings. The "brushes," labeled 1 and 2, make sliding contact with the rings to provide a path for the induced current to travel to an external circuit (not shown) connected to the brushes. The magnetic field has a left-to-right direction (from the north pole to the south pole) in the space between the magnets in the rotating coil figure. It is assumed that the coil has a constant speed of rotation.

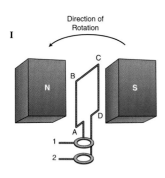

a) When the generator coil is in position I shown in the rotating coil is a current being generated? A current is produced if the wire cuts the magnetic field lines. Record your answer and the reason for your answer in your log.

b) Use a graph similar to the one shown below. Plot a point at the origin of the graph, indicating the amount of induced current is zero at the instant corresponding to the beginning of one rotation of the coil.

c) One-fourth turn later, at the instant when the rotating coil is in position II, is a current being generated? Record your answer and the reason for your answer in your log.

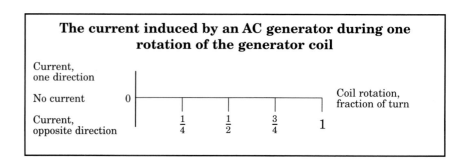

d) On your graph, plot a point directly above the $\frac{1}{4}$-turn mark at a height equal to the top of the vertical axis to represent maximum current flow in one direction.

The current induced by an AC generator during one rotation of the generator coil

Current, one direction

No current

Current, opposite direction

0

$\frac{1}{4}$ $\frac{1}{2}$ $\frac{3}{4}$ 1

Coil rotation, fraction of turn

✎ e) One-half turn into the rotation of the coil, at the instant shown in the rotating coil position III, the current again is zero because all sides of the coil are moving parallel to the magnetic field. Plot a point at the $\frac{1}{2}$ mark on the horizontal axis to show that no current is being induced at that instant.

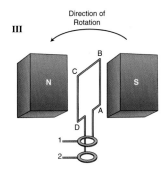

III Direction of Rotation

✎ f) At the instant at which $\frac{3}{4}$ of the rotation of the coil has been completed, shown by the rotating coil in position IV, the induced current again is maximum because coil sides AB and CD again are moving across the magnetic field at maximum rate. However, this is not exactly the same situation as shown in the rotating coil position II; it is a different situation in one important way: the direction of the induced current has reversed. Follow the directions of the arrows which represent the direction of the current flow in the coil to notice that, at this instant, the current would flow to an external circuit out of brush 2 and would return through brush 1. On your graph, plot a point below the $\frac{3}{4}$-turn mark at a distance as far below the horizontal axis as the bottom end of the vertical axis. This point will represent maximum current in the opposite, or "alternate," direction of the current shown earlier at $\frac{3}{4}$-turn.

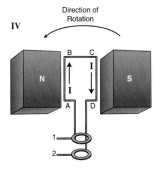

IV Direction of Rotation

✎ g) The rotating coil in position I is used again to show the instant at which one full rotation of the generator coil has been completed. Again, all sides of the coil are moving parallel to the magnetic field, and no current is being induced. Plot a point on the horizontal axis at the 1-turn mark to show that the current at this instant is zero.

5. You have plotted only 5 points to represent the current induced during one complete cycle of an AC generator.

✎ a) Where would the points that would represent the amount of induced current at each instant during one complete rotation of the generator coil be plotted?

✎ b) What is the overall shape of the graph? Should the graph be smooth, or have sharp edges? Sketch it to connect the points plotted on your graph.

✎ c) What would the graph look like for additional rotations of the generator coil, if the same speed and resistance in the external circuit were maintained.

DC Generator

6. Your teacher will explain and demonstrate a hand-operated, direct current (DC) generator. During the demonstration, make the observations needed to answer these questions:

a) When the DC generator is used to light a bulb, describe the brightness of the bulb when the generator is cranked slowly, and rapidly. Write your observations in your log.

b) When the DC generator is connected to a galvanometer, describe the action of the galvanometer needle when the generator is cranked slowly, and rapidly.

7. The diagram shows important parts of a DC generator. As in step 3, build a model of the generator to help you analyze how it works.

8. Use a graph similar to the one shown below. Complete the graph using the same pattern of analysis applied to the AC generator.

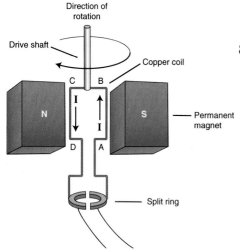

a) At the instant shown in the DC generator diagram, the induced current is maximum. The instant corresponds to the rotating coil II. Plot a point on the graph directly above the $\frac{1}{4}$-turn mark at a height equal to the top of the vertical axis to represent maximum current flow at that instant.

b) At the instant $\frac{1}{4}$-turn earlier than the instant shown in the DC generator figure, corresponding to the zero mark of rotation, the current would have been zero because all sides of the coil would have been moving parallel to the direction of the magnetic field. Therefore, plot a point at the origin of the graph.

c) Similarly, the induced current again would be zero at the instant $\frac{1}{4}$-turn later than the instant shown in the DC generator figure; therefore, plot a point on the horizontal axis at the $\frac{1}{2}$-turn mark.

The current induced by an AC generator during one rotation of the generator coil

Current

No current

0    $\frac{1}{4}$ $\frac{1}{2}$ $\frac{3}{4}$ 1   Coil rotation, fraction of turn

9. Notice the arrangement used to transfer current from the generator to the external circuit for the DC generator. It is different from the arrangement used for the AC generator. The DC generator has a "split-ring commutator" for transferring the current to the external circuit. Notice that if the coil shown in the DC generator figure were rotated $\frac{1}{4}$-turn in either direction, the "brush" ends that extend from the coil to make rubbing contact with each half of the split ring would reverse, or switch, the connection to the external circuit. Further, notice that the connection to the external circuit would be reversed at the same instant that the induced current in the coil reverses due to the change in direction in which the sides of the coil move through the magnetic field. The outcome is that while the current induced in the coil alternates, or changes direction each $\frac{1}{2}$-rotation, the current delivered to the external circuit always flows in the same direction. Current that flows always in one direction is called direct current, or DC.

a) Plot a point on the graph at a point directly above the $\frac{3}{4}$-turn mark at the same height as the point plotted earlier for the $\frac{1}{4}$-turn mark.

b) As done for the AC generator, find out how to connect the points plotted on this graph to represent the amount of current delivered always in the same direction to the external circuit during the entire cycle.

REFLECTING ON THE ACTIVITY AND THE CHALLENGE

It is time to begin preparing for the chapter challenge. Now that you know how a generator works, you should begin to think about toys that might generate electricity. You should also think about how you could assemble "junk" into a toy generator, or do some research on homemade generators and motors.

PHYSICS TO GO

1. What is the purpose of

    a) an electric generator?
    b) an electric motor?

2. How does a direct current differ from an alternating current? Use graphs to illustrate your answer.

3. In an electric generator, a wire is placed in a magnetic field. Under what conditions is a current generated?

STRETCHING EXERCISES

1. What is the meaning of "Hertz," abbreviated "Hz," often seen as a unit of measurement associated with electricity or stereo sound components such as amplifiers and speakers?

2. What does it mean to say that household electricity has a frequency of 60 Hz?

3. Have you ever heard 60 Hz AC being emitted from a fluorescent light or a transformer?

4. Look at a catalog or visit a store where sound equipment is sold, and check out the "frequency response" of speakers— what does it mean?

5. Hertz was a person, Heinrich Hertz, a 19th-century German physicist. Find out about the unit of measurement named after him, and write a brief report on what you find.

Activity Five
Building an Electric Motor

WHAT DO YOU THINK?

You plug a mixer into the wall and turn a switch and the mixer spins and spins—a motor is operating.

• How do you think the electricity makes the motor turn?

Write your answer to this question in your *Active Physics log*. Be prepared to discuss your ideas with your small group and other members of your class.

FOR YOU TO DO

1. Study the diagram on page H110 closely. Carefully assemble the materials, as shown in the diagram, to build a basic electric motor. Follow any additional directions provided by your teacher.

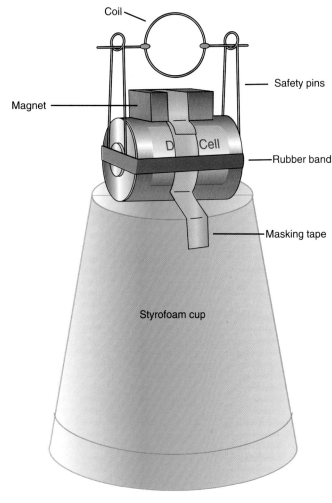

Coil

Safety pins

Magnet

D Cell

Rubber band

Masking tape

Styrofoam cup

2. When your motor is operating successfully, find as many ways as you can to make the motor change its direction of rotation.

a) Describe each way you tried and identify the ways that were successful.

3. Hold another magnet with your fingers and bring it near the coil from above, facing the original magnet, as the motor is operating.

a) Describe what happens. Does the orientation of the second magnet make a difference?

4. Replace the single magnet with a pair of attracting magnets on top of the battery.

a) What is the effect?

5. Think of other ways to change the speed of the motor. With the approval of your teacher, try out your methods.

a) Describe ways to change the speed of the motor.

6. Use a hand generator as the energy source instead of the battery. You can disconnect the battery without removing it from the structure by placing an insulating material, such as a piece of cardboard, between the safety pin and the battery to open the circuit at either end of the battery. Then clip the wires from the generator to the safety pins to deliver current from the generator to the motor.

a) Discuss what you find out.

FOR YOU TO READ

The history of science is filled with discoveries that have led to leaps of progress in knowledge and applications. This is certainly true of physics and, in particular, electricity and magnetism. These discoveries "favor" the prepared mind. Oersted's discovery in 1820 of the magnetic field surrounding a current-carrying wire already has been mentioned.

Michael Faraday

Similarly, Michael Faraday's discovered electromagnetic induction in 1831. Faraday was seeking a way to induce electricity using currents and magnets; he noticed that a brief induced current happened in one circuit when a nearby circuit was switched on and off. (How would that cause induction? Can you explain it?) Both Oersted and Faraday are credited for taking advantage of the events that happened before their eyes, and pursuing them.

About one-half century after Faraday's discovery of electromagnetic induction, which immediately led to development of the generator, another event occurred. In 1873 a Belgian engineer, Zénobe Gramme, was setting up DC generators to be demonstrated at an exposition (a forerunner of a "worlds fair") in Vienna, Austria. Steam engines were to be used to power the generators, and the electrical output of the generators would be demonstrated. While one DC generator was operating, Gramme connected it to another generator that was not operating. The shaft of the inactive generator began rotation—it was acting as an electric motor! Although Michael Faraday had shown as early as 1821 that rotary motion could be produced using currents and magnets, a "motor effect," nothing useful resulted from it. Gramme's discovery, however, immediately showed that electric motors could be useful. In fact, the electric motor was demonstrated at the very Vienna exposition where Gramme's discovery was made. A fake waterfall was set up to drive a DC generator using a paddle wheel arrangement, and the electrical output of the generator was fed to a "motor" (a generator running "backwards"). The motor was shown to be capable of doing useful work.

REFLECTING ON THE ACTIVITY AND THE CHALLENGE

Decision time about the challenge is approaching for your group. In this activity you built a very basic, working electric motor. This is an important part of the challenge. However, knowing how to build an electric motor is only part of the challenge. Your toy must be fascinating to children. You must also be able to explain how it works.

PHYSICS TO GO

1. Some electric motors use electromagnets instead of permanent magnets to create the magnetic field in which the coil rotates. In such motors, of course, part of the electrical energy fed to the motor is used to create and maintain the magnetic field. Similarly, electromagnets instead of permanent magnets are used in some generators; part of the electrical energy produced by the generator is used to energize the magnetic field in which the generator coil is caused to turn. What advantages and disadvantages would result from using electromagnets instead of permanent magnets in either a motor or generator?

2. Design three possible toys that use a motor or a generator or both. One of these may be what you will use for your project.

3. The motor/generator you submit for the chapter challenge must be built from inexpensive, common materials. Make a list of possible materials you could use to construct an electric motor.

4. In the grading criteria for the chapter challenge marks are assigned for clearly explaining how and why your motor/generator works in terms of basic principles of physics. Explain how an electric motor or generator operates.

Activity Six
Building a Motor/Generator Toy

WHAT DO YOU THINK?

You may have heard the following expression used before: "The difference between men and boys is the size of their toys."

• **What characteristics make an item a toy?**

Write your answer to this question in your *Active Physics log*. Be prepared to discuss your ideas with your small group and other members of your class.

FOR YOU TO DO

1. Confer within your group and between your group and your teacher about whether you will pursue, as a basis for the motor/generator kit for the assessment, the motor design presented in this activity, an alternate design, or both. Whatever design(s) your group chooses to pursue, you are encouraged to be creative. Most designs can be improved in some way or another by substituting materials or making other changes. There is no single "best way" to go about designing the motor/generator and making it function within a toy or to produce electrical energy from another form of energy. The best way for your group is the way that the group can get the job done.

   a) When you have decided on a design, submit your design to your teacher for approval.

2. In your group decide how you will make the motor/generator fascinating to children. You may wish to use some of the ideas you generated in answering the What Do You Think question.

   a) Record your ideas in your log.

   b) Describe and make a sketch of your final design, and submit it to your teacher for approval.

3. Use the design for a DC motor is shown in the diagram as a basis to begin your construction. It can be adapted, as required, for the chapter assessment, to power a toy. Also as required, the motor could be adapted to be driven "backwards" by an external energy source to function as a DC generator.

   [The motor design shown was adapted from the following public domain work: Educational Development Center, Inc., *Batteries and Bulbs II* (New York: McGraw-Hill, 1971), pp. 85-88.]

Cork

Clips

Thumb tacks

Straight pins

Tin can

Magnets

Enameled wire

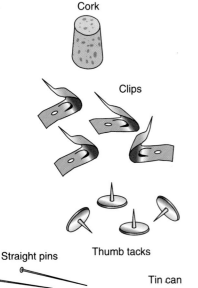

Thin stick

Wood

Masking tape

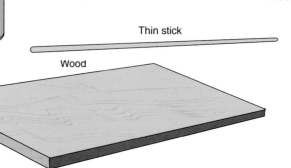

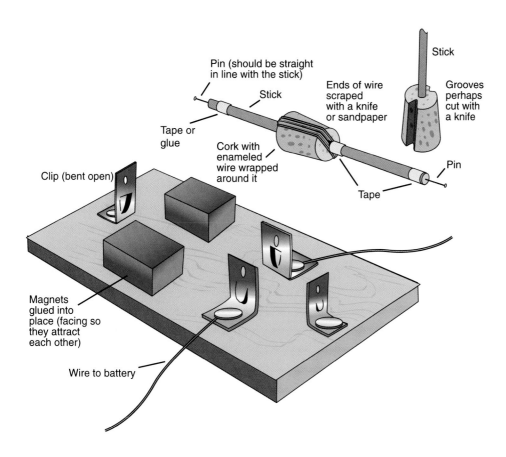

Pin (should be straight in line with the stick)

Stick

Tape or glue

Cork with enameled wire wrapped around it

Ends of wire scraped with a knife or sandpaper

Stick

Grooves perhaps cut with a knife

Pin

Tape

Clip (bent open)

Magnets glued into place (facing so they attract each other)

Wire to battery

REFLECTING ON THE ACTIVITY AND THE CHALLENGE

You are now well on your way to completing the chapter challenge. You have decided on the design for your motor/generator and the toy it will power.

PHYSICS TO GO

Your assignment is to prepare to meet the criteria of the assessment of the chapter challenge.

PHYSICS
AT WORK

Uriah Gilmore

HEADED FOR THE STARS

Uriah Gilmore loved to take electric appliances apart when he was growing up. "I couldn't always get them back together," he admits, "but I was so curious I couldn't help myself. I just had to see how they worked." Fortunately, Uriah's parents supported his curiosity.

Uriah and his fellow teammates from Cleveland, Ohio's East Technical High School recently won first place at the National High School Robotics Tournament at Epcot Center in Orlando, Florida for building a robot. "We were counseled along the way by engineers from NASA," he enthusiastically explains. "We called our robot Froggy and painted it green," Uriah continues, "and we used noisemakers so it even sounded like a frog." During the final contest "Froggy" was put in a pit with two other robots and had to place balls of a certain color in a specified area. The robot who got the most balls in won the contest.

"In my sophomore year the school closed and I went to East Technical High School which was the best thing that happened to me." He entered the engineering program and became a member of the engineering team—a team that is more popular than any sports team in his school.

Uriah enters Morehouse College this fall on a NASA scholarship. "But," he states, "it's not enough to be a good student. You also have to be involved with your school and your community." Uriah recently led a march on the Cleveland, Ohio City Hall to protest a law which threatens to fire certain teachers, including one who has inspired Uriah and was responsible for the revitalization of East Technical High School.

"My ultimate goal is to travel in space and explore the galaxy," he states. A shorter term goal is to be as involved in college as he has been in high school.

Chapter 3 Assessment

Your task is to prepare a kit of materials and instructions that a toy company will manufacture. Children will use these kits to make a motor or generator, or a combination electric motor/generator. It will serve both as a toy and to illustrate how the electric motors in home appliances work or how electricity can be produced from an energy source such as wind, moving water, a falling weight, or some other external source.

Review and remind yourself of the grading criteria that you and your classmates agreed on at the beginning of the chapter. The following was a suggested set of criteria.

- **(30%) The motor/generator is made from inexpensive, common materials, and the working parts are exposed.**

- **(40%) The instructions for the children clearly explain how to assemble and operate the motor/generator device, and explain how and why it works in terms of basic principles of physics.**

- **(30%) If used as a motor, the device will operate using a maximum of four 1.5 volt batteries (D cells), and will power a toy (such as a car, boat, crane, etc.) that will be fascinating to children.**

OR

- **(30%) If used as a generator, the device will demonstrate the production of electricity from an energy source such as wind, moving water, a falling weight, or some other external source and be fascinating to children.**

Physics You Learned

Motors

Generators

Galvanometers

Magnetic field from a current

Solenoids

Electromagnets

Induced currents

AC and DC generators

Index